BASIC ANTHROPOLOGY UNITS

GENERAL EDITORS
George and Louise Spindler
STANFORD UNIVERSITY

TECHNOLOGY
Strategies for Survival

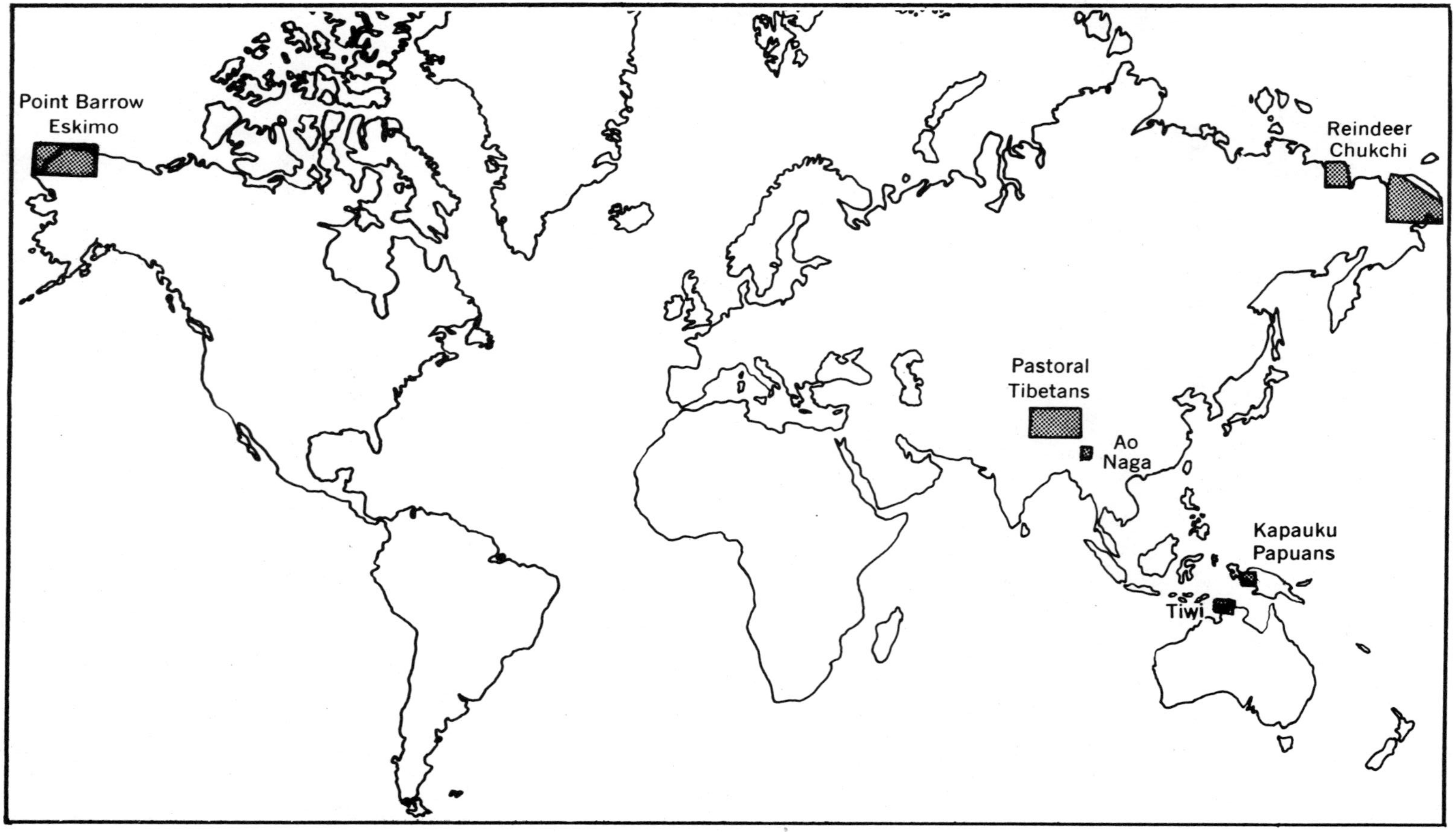
Point Barrow
Eskimo
Reindeer
Chukchi
Pastoral
Tibetans
Ao
Naga
Kapauku
Papuans
Tiwi

VERA LUSTIG-ARECCO

Technology
Strategies for Survival

HOLT, RINEHART AND WINSTON, INC.
New York   Chicago   San Francisco   Atlanta
Dallas   Montreal   Toronto   London   Sydney

GN
446
.L87

Library of Congress Cataloging in Publication Data

Lustig-Arecco, Vera.
Technology: strategies for survival.

(Basic anthropology units)
Bibliography: p. 74
1. Industries, Primitive. 2. Economics, Primitive.
I. Title.
GN446.L87   301.2′1   74-19342
ISBN 0-03-013496-X

Copyright © 1975 by Holt, Rinehart and Winston, Inc.
All rights reserved
Printed in the United States of America
5 6 7 8   059   9 8 7 6 5 4 3 2 1

To my parents

Foreword

THE BASIC ANTHROPOLOGY UNITS

Basic Anthropology Units are designed to introduce students to essential topics in the contemporary study of man. In combination they have greater depth and scope than any single textbook. They may also be assigned selectively to cover topics relevant to the particular profile of a given course, or they may be utilized separately as authoritative guides to significant aspects of anthropology.

Many of the Basic Anthropology Units serve as the point of intellectual departure from which to draw on the Case Studies in Cultural Anthropology and Case Studies in Education and Culture. This integration is designed to enable instructors to utilize these easily available materials for their instructional purposes. The combination introduces flexibility and innovation in teaching and avoids the constraints imposed by the encyclopedic textbook. To this end, selected Case Studies have been annotated in each unit. Questions and exercises are also provided as suggestive leads for instructors and students toward productive engagements with ideas and data in other sources as well as the Case Studies.

This series was planned over a period of several years by a number of anthropologists, some of whom are authors of the separate Basic Units. The completed series will include units representing all the basic sectors of contemporary anthropology, including archeology, biological anthropology, and linguistics, as well as the various subfields of social and cultural anthropology.

THE AUTHOR

Originally from Argentina, Vera Lustig-Arecco holds a Master of Arts degree in anthropology from the University of California at Los Angeles, where she has been advanced to candidacy for the doctoral degree. She taught cultural anthropology at California State College, Dominguez Hills, and has done field work among the Huichol Indians of Mexico and a North Athapaskan group, the Chandalar Kutchin. Based on her research in Alaska she has published an article on the modernization process, measured by the differential technological adoptions of several households. Her interests include material culture, acculturation, innovation, and cultural ecology with a primary concern for the integration of biological with cultural variables.

THIS UNIT

Probably no significant area of human behavior has been more seriously neglected by contemporary ethnography than material culture. In this Basic Unit, titled *Technology: Strategies for Survival,* Lustig-Arecco applies to the analysis of material culture the taxonomy and concepts only recently developed by Wendell Oswalt in *Habitat and Technology: The Evolution of Hunting* (1973) in order to understand the technoeconomic adaptation of not only hunting, but also of pastoralist and farming societies. The terminology that she uses will be new and challenging. However, the reader will soon find that once the elements of the conceptual structure are mastered, and the author has proceeded in such a way that this mastery is easy to achieve, the study of the material culture will, for the first time, become meaningful and exciting.

No aspect of human life has played a more significant role in human evolution than material culture broadly conceived within an economic context as a major mode of adaptation. The complexities of the human brain are intimately linked with tool use and language, and, as Lustig-Arecco points out, so are certain cognitive characteristics, such as the anticipation of the future and deferred gratification, which she suggests are functionally related to tool use.

Though the author does not presume to take the step, it is clear that the kinds of understandings that begin to emerge with the application of a systematic conceptual structure of this sort to technological form and process may be applied to our contemporary situation. The analysis of material culture is particularly relevant in this age when the material consequences of our technoeconomic adaptation seem about to smother us, both in a literal and a figurative sense.

George and Louise Spindler
General Editors
PORTOLA VALLEY, CALIF.

Preface

In an age of technological profusion and confusion, it may seem anachronistic to write about the material culture of preliterate peoples. Social relationships, religious institutions, and political alignments have undoubtedly played a role in man's efforts to survive. Yet the key adaptive mode of our human ancestors was the increased efficiency of the material forms they made. Because it is the nature of man to wonder about his past and because the foundations of culture are technological, this study focuses on those manufactures that have led to the survival of highly diverse peoples.

The societies selected for this comparative study represent major economic levels and a broad geographical and ecological diversity. Whenever possible, peoples included in the Case Studies in Cultural Anthropology (Holt, Rinehart and Winston, Inc.) are utilized. The source ethnographies are historically comparable, as they were all collected soon after the societies whose lifeways are described were contacted by Western civilizations. Another consideration was to include only peoples lacking structured political organizations. Thus the foragers, pastoralists, and farmers treated in this book were autonomous, stateless people ruled primarily by kin-based institutions.

V. L.-A.

Acknowledgements

In essence, this study was possible because of the efforts of conscientious ethnographers who painstakingly collected innumerable details on the behavior and materials of untouched groups of men. I am largely indebted to the authors of the publications I have used and to those whose work I could not include here but who provided me with the satisfaction of knowing that further analysis may be carried out. Wendell Oswalt's *Habitat and Technology* (1973) provided the basic units of analysis. I am deeply grateful to him for his teachings and guidance, and although I have altered the focus of his approach slightly, the responsibility for the treatment of the materials is all mine. I am also very grateful to Johannes Wilbert, who introduced me to anthropology. With great pleasure I thank my sister, Lidia, for her many helpful and insightful editorial suggestions. Gratitude is a poor substitute for my husband's encouragement and patience during the writing of this book.

Contents

Foreword   vii

Preface   ix

Acknowledgements   xi

Introduction   1
   Plan of the Unit, 2

1. Taxonomy and Concepts   5

2. Foragers   10
   Tiwi, 10
      Technoeconomic Adaptation, 11
      Storants, 14
      Analysis, 14
   Point Barrow Eskimo, 16
      Technoeconomic Adaptation, 17
      Storants, 23
      Analysis, 23
   How to Use the Subsistant Taxonomy and the Technotask Approach to Material Culture, 27
   Case Study Interactions, 30

3. Pastoralists   31
   Pastoral Tibetans, 31
      Technoeconomic Adaptation, 31
      Storants, 36
      Analysis, 36
   Reindeer Chukchi, 38
      Technoeconomic Adaptation, 38
      Storants, 42
      Analysis, 43
   Case Study Interactions, 46

4. Farmers 47
    Ao Naga, 47
        Technoeconomic Adaptation, 48
        Storants, 52
        Analysis, 53
    Kapauku Papuans, 55
        Technoeconomic Adaptation, 56
        Storants, 62
        Analysis, 63
    Case Study Interactions, 66

5. Foragers, Pastoralists, and Farmers Compared 67

Glossary 72

References 74

Relevant Case Studies 76

Introduction

Technology has long been recognized as playing a prominent role in man's efforts to survive. Since the beginnings of human time, hands, teeth, and feet were used to obtain food. Millenia must have gone by before men realized that the task could be made more efficient with the aid of sticks or stones. These natural objects, which will be called *naturefacts*, were extracted from their context and used without modification. This discovery did not involve any processual skills nor great intellectual capabilities. Our earliest ancestors probably killed wild animals with unmodified sticks or stones which they used only once. A long familiarity with naturefacts presumably led to their purposeful modification. A stick used to dig roots became more efficient when one end was sharpened and a chipped stone was a remarkable improvement on the natural model. These incipient artifacts will be called *preartifacts* because they required minimal craft skills and processing time and were probably discarded after one or two usages. True *artifacts*, manufactured later, required greater processing knowledge, and became the first permanent human possessions.

The caloric requirements of aboriginal men were obtained with the naturefacts and artifacts that enabled the direct procurement of food, and will be called *subsistants*. The definition excludes weapons and other objects used for any purposes besides food procurement. Thus, a bow and arrow is a subsistant when a hunter shoots a deer for consumption but it is not a subsistant when employed in sports and ritual contexts. With the domestication of animals and plants, the range of available resources increased, as well as man's control over the environment. Tending domestic animals and preparing the soil for cultivation became additional food-procuring measures, requiring the extension of the subsistant concept to include the material objects employed during the performance of these tasks.

Sometimes preliterate peoples also depended on the storage of gathered edibles to survive. Although foragers did not typically store food, quite a few societies did. Reasonably important among pastoralists who moved often and only killed their animals at indicated times, storing became crucial for the survival of farmers who depended on seasonal harvests. Storing devices, however, must not have been as important where root crops grew since these plants were collected often. The storing forms will be termed *storants* and, like the subsistants, they will be classified as natural or man-made. The subsistants and storants will be compared on the basis of their *components*, the discrete functional parts that make up each form. For example, a relatively simple spear may be visualized as having three components: a stone head, a wood shaft, and a fiber cord binding the head to the shaft. Decorative elaborations are disregarded when they are not functionally essential.

To facilitate their subsistence pursuits, aboriginal foragers, herders, and farmers employed natural and artificial forms in intimate association with the subsistants. These will be given the general label of *aids* and, suggestively, the prototypes from which the subsistants evolved were the natural aids. Hands, still used by contemporary primitives to gather plants, are considered aids and not subsistants because they are not material forms yet they enable the direct procurement of food. In many cases, two subsistants were employed together to accomplish one task, such as when a dam was placed in a river to restrain the movement of fish which were later caught with leisters or fish spears. An *association* is defined by the employment of two or more forms: either two subsistants or a combination of subsistants and aids to fulfill one subsistence task. An example from plant cultivation is a plow, the aid used to prepare the soil, and a sickle, the subsistant with which the harvest is obtained. Another example is the association between a canoe aid paddled by a northern hunter in search of caribou and the subsistant spear which kills the animal.

The functional counterpart of the association is the task. Both concepts are linked, resulting in a more comprehensive unit which will be called a *technotask*. In the last example above, the technotask refers to the caribou search and the material means employed to obtain the animal, that is, the canoe and spear. Another subsistence task performed by northern hunters is the shooting of ducks. Duck and caribou hunting represent functional units of the activity category "to hunt" (Fig. 1). The technotask concept provides the organizing guidelines of this book because it emphasizes the functional aspects of man's survival technology. The subsistants are described in the context in which they were used. The economic variability between foragers, pastoralists, and farmers will be assessed according to their technotasks, thus emphasizing their different employment of the survival materials.

PLAN OF THE UNIT

The taxonomy and concepts are introduced in the first chapter. Precise guidelines on the application of the approach are offered at the end of the second chapter, which describes the technotasks of foragers. The guidelines are intended to help the student utilize these concepts when analyzing the survival strategies of other societies. In the subsequent comprehensive chart (Table 5, Chapter 2) the units of analysis are arranged hierarchically with particular examples from the section on the Tiwi. This chart contains all the elements on which the comparisons between subsistants and technotasks are based.

The three chapters dealing with particular peoples (see frontispiece map) include introductory sentences, a main section on the focal survival activities deter-

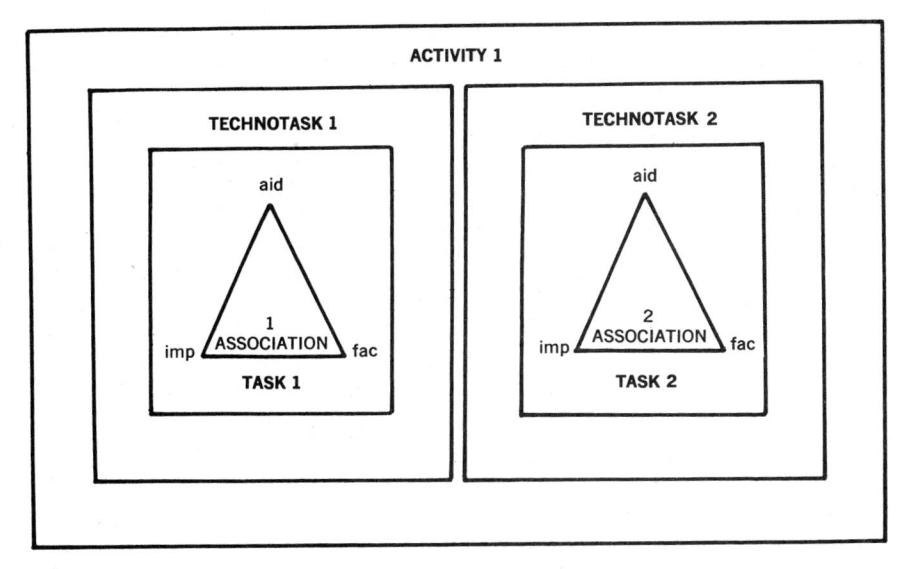

Figure 1. Diagrammatic representation of the units of analysis and their hierarchical relationships (imp = implement, fac = facility; both are subsistant classes). An association represents the use of subsistants and aids whereas a task is the functional context in which the association takes place. Together, associations and tasks form a technotask. Two or more technotasks include all the materials and tasks within one activity. For example: the Tiwi gathered plants (Task 1) using a digging stick (implement) and their hands (aid) in association (Association 1). The Tiwi also gathered shellfish (Task 2) with a stick (subsistant) and their hands (aid) in another association (Association 2). Both plant and shellfish gathering represent tasks in the activity "to gather" (Activity I).

mined by their associations, a consideration of storants, and an analytical summary. In the main section of the chapters, the survival strategies are described following a summary description of the associations divided by activity. The economic activity which supplies a greater proportion of the group's food supply is listed first and the others follow according to their decreasing productive importance. In the tabular summaries at the beginning of each section, the technotasks are identified by the subsistants and aids listed in the order of use. The subsistants only are italicized whereas in the text which follows, all the forms in the association are placed in italics. Some subsistants are used alone. These are listed at the beginning of each section, separated by a line from the associations, and are described in the text where relevant. All the subsistants and storants for each society are represented in tables near the end of the respective chapters. In many cases, one or several varieties of a subsistant type were manufactured. The variety with most components is listed in the table and described in the text, while the number of alternatives is recorded in parentheses, after the type.

In the analytical summary at the end of each chapter, the selected group of foragers, pastoralists, and farmers are compared on the basis of their subsistant and storant inventories and their technotasks in hopes of achieving a detailed understanding of their survival strategies and the technoeconomic adaptation of each level of sociocultural development. The last chapter is followed by a glossary of all the technical terms used.

1
Taxonomy and Concepts

Anthropologists commonly correlate tool manufacture with an increase in human brain size. A causal relationship is also suspected since one is presumed to have reinforced the other in evolutionary developments. Culture selected for bigger brains, which in turn selected for a more complex culture. If linguistic expression and tool manufacture depend to a large extent on the structure of the brain, then language and technology possibly developed along parallel lines. In his work on the evolutionary development of language, Hockett (1960) suggested that the capacity of protohominids and lower animals to refer to objects or situations not immediately present either in space or time was based on the feature of displacement. The capacity for displaced thought marked the beginnings of language, called by Hockett the prelanguage stage. In conceptual terms, displacement came closest to the application of foresight evidenced in man when he began to make preartifacts. Thus, prelanguage could have logically preceded the preartifactual stage of technology. It has been proven that chimpanzees are endowed with the capacity for displacement and for tool making. They may, consequently, be considered to be at an equivalent stage to the human prelanguage or preartifactual condition best identified by the absence of variability in processing techniques.

Presumably, during their evolutionary development, language and technology continued to reinforce and stimulate each other with the intellectual capabilities preceding manual skills. The efficiency of language increased greatly when our hominid ancestors became capable of combining minimal vocal sounds or phonemes to produce different meaningful symbols according to their relative placement in utterances. Linguists label these units of meaning as "morphemes" and they possess a property, called duality of patterning by Hockett, illustrated by the English morphemes "tap," "pat," and "apt," in which the meaning of the word changes through the permutation of three intrinsically meaningless sounds. Hockett considered that this capacity marked the emergence of true language. But how, one may ask, could this discovery have affected technology? Duality of patterning became a distinguishing characteristic of *Homo sapiens*, and when he had this feature well under control, he learned that symbols could be joined in different ways to communicate thoughts efficiently. Since the possession of language offers possibilities for innovation, it is not farfetched to suppose that our ancestors transferred the concept of elementary combinations to the materials they handled, and found that if they joined two parts and later bound them with a third, they had increased the efficiency of their manufactures. Further handling may have led to the discovery that the conjunction of components allowed their rearrangement, resulting in a diversity of forms to fulfill different functions. Based on the feature of duality of patterning, the range and efficiency of language and technology increased and, suggestively at this point, true artifacts began to be made. Thus, we might say that after prelanguage became true language, preartifacts became true artifacts, and hominids became men.

The subsistant concept is only briefly introduced in this unit since detailed definitions may be found in Oswalt's *Habitat and Technology* (1973). Nevertheless, the main classificatory divisions will be outlined, and their explicit and implicit meanings discussed. The guiding criteria are primarily functional and structural, yet evolutionary and conceptual implications are also presented. For the sake of clarity, the preartifacts are not added as a separate class, but incorporated with the artifacts which, together with the naturefacts, represent the basic subsistant dichotomy: the forms merely removed from context and those modified prior to use. All the classes to be introduced belong either in one or the other group. The subsistants used to obtain plant or animal foods are divided into implements and facilities, primarily based on their function (Table 1). A subsistant is called an *implement* when it requires the direct exertion of human energy to obtain plant or animal foods. This classificatory dichotomy has significant implications. For example, in a study on the selective adaptation of human anatomy, Alice Brues (1959) found a close correlation between the main food-procuring artifact used by a group and the average body build. She discovered that a primary dependence on the hoe gave selective advantage to medium-built, sturdy physiques. The hoe, a digging stick, or any other implement used to collect immobile species, such as plants, are classified by Oswalt as *instruments*. Thus, it may be hypothesized that societies which depended heavily on instruments to procure their food possessed stocky builds. Oswalt defines *weapons* as implements which injure or kill the moving prey, like clubs, spears, or bows and arrows. Earlier, Brues had found a significant association between certain groups of people and their degree of utilization of each of these forms. The extensive use of bludgeoning implements, such as clubs, favored large bodies, whereas spears were more effective among peoples with linear builds, and bows and arrows were predominantly employed by short, broad-shouldered men.

By contrast with implements, *facilities* are primarily stationary devices that passively await the prey and do not require muscular energy to function; nor do they harvest plant products. These forms attract, contain, hold, or restrain the animal prey. Because of their stationary nature, physical correlates are probably harder, if at all possible, to determine. When a man's presence is necessary for a facility to function, it is a *tended set*, like a fishing rod and line, but if it works in the absence of men, like a corral in which domesticated herds are kept, it is an *untended set*. All subsistants are further regarded as simple or complex depending on their structural characteristics. Whereas *simple forms* do not change in appearance while being employed, and may consist of only one part, *complex subsistants* are defined by the dynamic relationship of their two or more component parts that

TABLE 1. SUBSISTANT TAXONOMY*

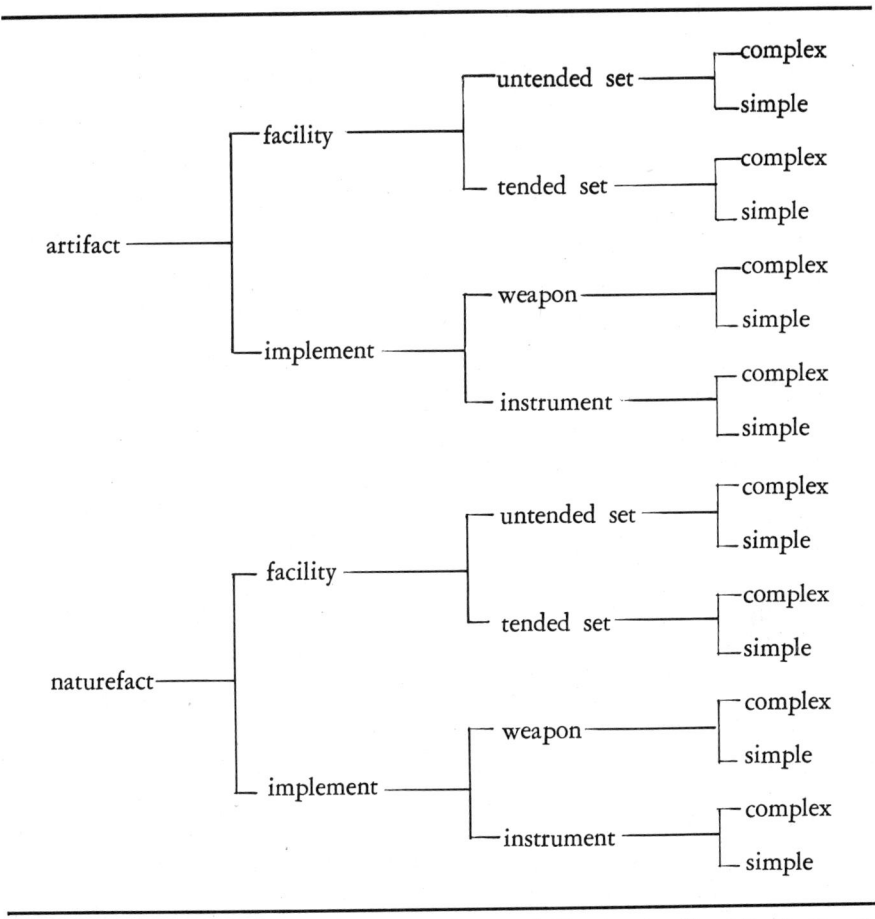

```
artifact ─┬─ facility ──┬─ untended set ──┬─ complex
          │             │                 └─ simple
          │             └─ tended set ────┬─ complex
          │                               └─ simple
          └─ implement ─┬─ weapon ────────┬─ complex
                        │                 └─ simple
                        └─ instrument ────┬─ complex
                                          └─ simple

naturefact ─┬─ facility ──┬─ untended set ──┬─ complex
            │             │                 └─ simple
            │             └─ tended set ────┬─ complex
            │                               └─ simple
            └─ implement ─┬─ weapon ────────┬─ complex
                          │                 └─ simple
                          └─ instrument ────┬─ complex
                                            └─ simple
```

* From *Habitat and Technology: The Evolution of Hunting* by Wendell H. Oswalt. Copyright © 1973 by Holt, Rinehart and Winston, Inc. Reprinted by permission of Holt, Rinehart and Winston, Inc.

function through the application of a mechanical principle, as in the case of a harpoon.

The storants are also divided like the subsistants into natural and artificial categories (Table 2). Based on structural and functional criteria, storants are called *receptacles* when they closely confine food products, such as a pottery vessel, and *structures* when they serve other purposes besides food storage and the food is loosely held, such as inside a tent. Storants are labelled *short-term* when they contain food only temporarily, such as a leaf used to keep meat for a few days, to differentiate them from the *long-term* containers in which food is stored for longer periods as exemplified by rice granaries.

The hierarchical positions of the subsistant, as well as the storant units within

TABLE 2. STORANT TAXONOMY

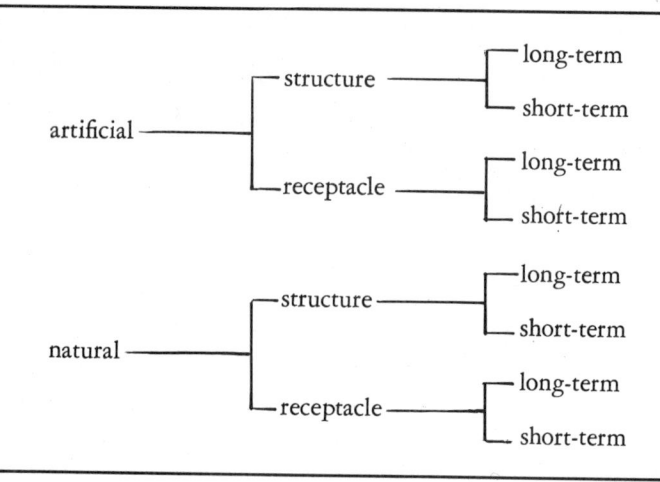

```
                    ┌─ structure ──┬─ long-term
                    │              └─ short-term
    artificial ─────┤
                    │              ┌─ long-term
                    └─ receptacle ─┴─ short-term

                    ┌─ structure ──┬─ long-term
                    │              └─ short-term
    natural ────────┤
                    │              ┌─ long-term
                    └─ receptacle ─┴─ short-term
```

the taxonomies, represent evolutionary levels. In the case of the subsistants, implements are presumed to have been used before the facilities, which did not require direct energy expenditures to work. Instruments, almost always used to obtain plants, were probably fashioned earlier than weapons, since collecting immobile food was relatively easier than killing moving prey. A supportive finding is that most instruments were made with only one component whereas some weapons became quite complex. The concept of setting up a form to function unattended was a significant cultural advance; therefore tended subsistants are considered simpler than the untended sets.

In addition to evolutionary statements, the subsistant taxonomy offers other insights about the nature of technology. Our understanding of the evolution of subsistant forms may profit from a reflection on the nontechnological aspects of material innovation. Implicit in the alternative usage of implements and facilities was a different appreciation of time. No significant time lapse occurred between the use of implements and the obtainment of food. But time did transpire between setting a facility and obtaining the prey. The development of the concept of time may have been intimately related to man's awareness of the spatial separation of the basic resources. At some point in his intellectual development, he must have realized that in order to tap his food resources more efficiently, his family had to forage in different places at the same time. Much later, he must have become aware of an extra-somatic alternative, perhaps when he began to use natural features such as pits or cliffs to trap the incoming prey. The different appreciation of time when employing facilities rather than implements may have given rise to the key economic concept of long-range results. Furthermore, the possession of long-term storants may have preceded or accompanied the use of facilities. Thus, after *Homo sapiens* realized that his needs could be more efficiently fulfilled if he learned to wait, the stage was set for the further elaborations of economic behavior.

Collective enterprises must have been organized after our ancestors began to depend on animal food. During his cultural beginnings, man appears to have led a plant-gathering existence and cooperation was probably not necessary, for each individual could harvest his own food. But after man began to depend on meat, he employed facilities designed strictly for animal prey, and when a community made a fence in which to restrain large game animals, planning, cooperation, and organization in subsistence activities must have been well under way. Possibly, these behavioral traits became selectively adaptive when man began to depend heavily on game, which may have taken place after his increasing dependence on facilities. It is generally accepted that our earliest ancestors had strong group ties and a division of labor based on the female reproductive cycle. The men were the hunters, primarily because the women had a more limited spatial mobility due to their child-rearing obligations. Thus, the purposeful planning, organization, and cooperation required to make and use a large facility were cultural developments on at least two biosocial needs: that of kinship solidarity and the differentiation of tastes.

In the case of people who depended on animal husbandry, the survival requirements differed from those of the earliest hunters for whom seeing an animal was one step removed from killing it. The capacity to wait must have been long established before man could have domesticated animals for future consumption. The notion of the passage of time was intimately related to the patience required by the hunters who waited for the animals to come to their traps and the pastoralists who tended their stock.

Patience was more clearly a necessary precondition for agriculture than for animal domestication. From the time the seed was sown until a crop was harvested, several months must have passed. Additional preconditions for plant domestication were sedentariness and territoriality. While surviving primarily with implements, hominids roamed over wide spaces, but when permanent structures were used to capture animals, the foragers had to return to the same region. Thus, after large facilities were built, at least seasonal settlements, which were possible because greater numbers of animals (needed to support sedentary populations) could be obtained with facilities than implements, became established. And since facilities were set up and used wherever game was known to be abundant and reliable, the beginnings of territoriality must have accompanied their use. The concept of territoriality is also essential to the cultivation of plants. Thus, the conceptual threshold that separated foraging from domestication must have been crossed by the time the first facilities were employed.

2
Foragers[1]

TIWI

The often-cited simplicity of aboriginal Australian material culture is attributed by ethnographers to physical isolation and insufficient resources. The Tiwi of Melville and Bathurst islands were separated from the mainland by only 30 miles of water, but they did not have any sustained contact with other aborigines. Yet the lack of complexity of their manufactures may not be attributed to a poverty of resources, since the near 2000 Tiwi obtained abundant and diverse wild foods the year round. The Tiwi were considered to be a single tribe with several loose territorial bands and no permanent settlements. The social and economic unit was the household, which included a man, his wives, their parents, children, and other relatives. Women collected the plant staples, making it desirable for a household head to have as many females as possible. The overwhelming importance of the women as food producers may have given rise to the unique system of marriage by which one man could acquire a large number of wives through a variety of means. Men with many wives became camp leaders with considerable authority over other men.

The Tiwi had quite a rich ceremonial life and the most elaborate ceremonies centered around the initiation of youths. When a boy was 14 years old, he left his parents' household and became an apprentice of the tribal elders until he reached 20 years of age. This custom resulted in the removal of all young males from the productive core. The reasons behind such remarkable behavior might have been the secondary economic roles of the males or the power of the older men who by this means eliminated the young competing suitors. Funeral ceremonies were only held for male leaders, and took place when their wives and relatives had accumulated large quantities of food, ceremonial paraphernalia, spears, and burial posts. The contrast between the extremely simple survival technology and the elaborateness of the ceremonial manufactures is striking. The spears and graveposts made for the funeral feasts symbolized wealth and status and differed in size, ornamentation, and paint. The implicit reasons for these ceremonies were the distribution of food among the less affluent guests, and the reinforcement of

---

[1] Details on the Tiwi material culture were obtained from the following sources: Basedow (1913), Goodale (1971), and B. Spencer (1914). Murdoch (1892) provided all the basic data on the Point Barrow Eskimo.

the marriage system, since the large quantities of food required could only be amassed through the possession of many wives.

Technoeconomic Adaptation

Famines were never recorded in the exceptionally bountiful environment of Melville and Bathurst islands. The Tiwi divided their subsistence activities by sex, according to the main habitats exploited. Thus women generally collected land foods whereas the men specialized in hunting air or water species. The staple was the plants gathered by the women while only a few animals were eaten, hunted by both sexes.

Gathering

plant gathering: *digging stick*/hands
shellfish gathering: *collecting stone* (crab-pulling stick)/hands
turtle-egg gathering: turtle-egg probe/hands
honey gathering: ladder/ax/*honey-removal stick*

The multiple females in a household gathered a large variety of edible plants growing among the profuse island vegetation. The staple foods were cycad nuts and a species of wild yam which the women and children dug up with their *digging sticks*. A woman collected the harvest in a bark basket which she supported on her back with a pole. Besides gathering vegetable foods, the women picked up reptiles with their hands and, occasionally, collected shellfish with any available *sticks* or *stones*. Sometimes they captured a crab by teasing it with a *stick* which the animal eventually grabbed. The women also located turtle eggs in the sand with long *stick probes* and reached honey deposits on high trees using branches as *ladders*. A woman cut down a nest with an *ax* and extracted the honey using a *brush* made by chewing one end of a fan-palm stalk until the fibers spread (Fig. 2).

Hunting

turtle, crocodile, dugong hunting: canoe/bailer/*spear* (club)
joint wallaby hunting: fire/beater sticks/*spear* (club)
bandicoot hunting: dingo/tree probe/ax/hands/*club*
opossum hunting 1: fire/*club*
opossum hunting 2: sticks and stones/*club*
opossum hunting 3: ladder/tree probe/hands
opossum hunting 4: ladder/tree probe/ax/*club*

club
throwing sticks
missile stones

The animal proteins procured by the men did not represent a significant portion of the diet. Occasionally, when on turtle, crocodile, or dugong hunting expeditions, six to eight men carried a bark *canoe* to a river and only two continued. One propelled the canoe and the other extracted the water with a mussel *bailer*. When the game was spotted, he killed it with a *spear*. The variety of spears was great, corre-

12 FORAGERS

Figure 2. Tiwi woman gathering honey inside a fallen log. (Courtesy of Arnold R. Pilling, Wayne State University.)

sponding to that of clubs and throwing sticks. In general, spears resembled javelins in shape, size, and weight (Fig. 3). Many were grooved or fluted longitudinally and decorated with ocher. The most elaborate examples had a long, sharp point and 10 to 30 backward pointing barbs on one or both sides of the shaft, behind which 4 to 8 serrations projected at right angles to the shaft. Despite this apparent complexity, all spears were made of a single piece of wood (Fig. 4).

The wet season was an unattractive time to hunt, as the grass grew tall, providing effective cover both for animal prey and poisonous snakes. When the rains stopped, a senior man of a district organized the first burning of the grasses, to open the hunting season. The joint wallaby hunt was the only activity that involved Tiwi of both sexes and all ages. The "boss" of a district invited 10 to 15 related household heads to supervise the younger hunters who set the grass on *fire* over a large area. Meanwhile, the women and children rounded up the dazed animals with *beater sticks* and the younger men slaughtered wallaby with *spears* or *clubs*. The search for bandicoots also followed the opening of the hunting season. These were the only animals hunted by the women, with the aid of specially trained *dingoes*. When a sleeping bandicoot was located inside a hollow log, the woman inserted a quickly trimmed *branch* to locate the animal. With an *ax*, she cut a hole in the log, retrieved the marsupial with her *hands*, and killed it with a *club*.

In Tiwiland there were more alternative ways to take opossum than to perform any other activity. The simplest method was to light a *fire* at the base of a hollow log to drive the animal out with smoke. After its exit, it was killed with a *club*.

Figure 3. Tiwi man holding hunting spears. (Courtesy of Arnold R. Pilling, Wayne State University.)

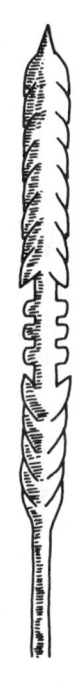

Figure 4. Tiwi spear made of one piece of wood. (From Australian Aboriginal *by Herbert Basedow. Copyright 1925 by F. W. Preece and Sons.)*

If an opossum slept inside a hollow branch of a live tree, the hunter either felled the animal with *sticks and stones* and then *clubbed* it to death, or he climbed the tree with the aid of a stick used as *ladder*, and by inserting a *trimmed branch* into the opening he checked the animal's presence. He took out the opossum with his *hands* and struck it against the tree. The most technologically involved alternative occurred when an opossum was deep within a branch. The hunter, after climbing with the fashioned *ladder* and checking the animal's location with a *probe*, either enlarged the opening with his *ax*, or chopped off the branch, alerting the people below to pursue the animal, which was then killed with a *club*.

An unusual technological occurrence was the Tiwi employment both of a naturefact and an artifact to accomplish the same task. Besides manufacturing *clubs*, the Tiwi usually picked up natural sticks from the ground and used them to kill sleeping iguanas or carpet snakes. Unmodified and manufactured sticks were also thrown at wallabies and flying foxes resting on mangrove branches, or geese that flew by. *Throwing sticks* usually lay in bundles around a camp and were picked up by any man leaving in a hurry. Other natural weapons were *stones* thrown by the boys at the abundant birds.

Fishing

mangrove fishing: canoe/bailer/*spear*

Despite reports that abundant and various fish species lived in the surrounding waters, hardly any mention of fishing could be found in the ethnographies. Basedow (1925) mentioned a *fish spear* thrust from a *canoe* and Goodale (1957) reported that a club was used in mangrove swamps. The confusion stems from the fact that throwing sticks, spears, and clubs formed a graded series and it was difficult to distinguish between the types. The lengths of the weapons and the number of barbs, when present, serve as classificatory guidelines. Clubs and throwing sticks measured from 1 to 6 feet with an average number of 6 barbs, while spears, measuring from 7 to 13 feet had an average of 14 barbs. B. Spencer (1914) also reported a vegetable-fiber binding around the shaft of clubs and spears. But the vine did not join two parts since all examples were made of one piece of wood. Therefore, the binder must have been decorative.

Storants

The ethnographic report that crocodile meat was inedible after two or three days suggests that the island climate was unfavorable for long-term food storage although food was stored for short periods. One of the simplest and most ingenious storing techniques was to mark—with a stick—a turtle egg or honey deposit. Four other storants were used, but all for very short periods of time and mostly during ceremonies. The storing of cycad nuts was associated with processing, since after treating the nuts with water to remove their fatal poison, the Tiwi carried them to a swamp and placed them inside cycad leaves for almost three days prior to their consumption. One episode in the initiation ceremonies included placing yams on a grass bed made on a swamp, to remove them on a later day and place them on the dry ground, where the yams were protected from the sun with a cover of branches. Apart from the ceremonial occasions, yams were stored in bark baskets made by the women.

Analysis

A review of the Tiwi survival equipment and strategies brings out one recurrent theme: their almost unsurpassed simplicity. The Tiwi fulfilled their most basic survival needs with only twelve subsistants, six naturefacts, and six artifacts. In the first chapter general evolutionary statements were offered, based on the relative employment of naturefacts and artifacts, and it was suggested that before artifacts were manufactured, naturefacts were probably used in subsistence activities. The fact that half the Tiwi subsistant inventory consisted in naturefacts points to the rudimentary character of their technology. The subsistant table includes a structural division of simple and complex forms based on whether or not their component parts moved during use. The complex subsistants were postulated to be more advanced than the simple productions, but no Tiwi material object, whether subsistant or nonsubsistant, was complex. That the mechanization principle and all facilities were unknown are, perhaps, the most remarkable aspects of their technology.

How can the absence of complex subsistants and facilities be explained? In general, aboriginal foragers used or manufactured few complex instruments, but complex weapons were relatively common. Therefore, one may reasonably expect the Tiwi to have possessed at least one complex weapon, especially since the spear and spear thrower were among the most characteristic Australian manufactures. But even this ubiquitous subsistant was not made. Since the women gathered the staple with instruments, the absence of complex weapons and facilities might be due to their relative uselessness in Tiwiland, particularly because of the availability of simple weapons to kill the few animals hunted. Moreover, throughout the world, complex implements seem to have been predominantly used by men, which helps to explain why the Tiwi did not possess any, as their staple was procured by the women. Additionally, the use of facilities usually requires the passage of time between the setting of a form and the capturing of game. Such protracted techniques could have been impractical and unnecessary in an environment where foods were immediately available. Apparently, immediacy in all survival activities was a Tiwi characteristic.

Each naturefact and artifact was considered to be made up of a certain number of elementary parts or components. The total component count of the Tiwi subsistants was very small: only fifteen were recorded and the most complex was the ax, used primarily to gather food and secondarily as an aid. B. Spencer (1914) considered it to be the crudest found in Austrialia for it consisted in a hafted, flaked sandstone tool. All the other Tiwi subsistants were one component sticks or stones.

A structurally simple material culture does not result in a functionally complex technology. Given the extreme simplicity of Tiwi subsistants, few alternative usages are expected. Essentially, the Tiwi survival inventory was represented by a multipurpose form—a stick, sometimes used as an instrument to collect various species of food, as a club to hit an animal, or as a projectile to throw at birds. In functional terms, only two basic methods were applied. Either the subsistants were hand held, such as the stone to collect mussels or they were projected as missiles, exemplified by the spears and throwing sticks.

The storants were only temporarily employed and no long-term devices were known, which is congruent with the elementary nature of the technoeconomic pattern. According to Berndt and Berndt (1964) Australian aborigines did not store because their foods did not keep. It is noteworthy that the Tiwi mostly stored collected plants. No reference is made of meat being stored, perhaps reflecting the differential decomposing characteristics of plants and animals. But perhaps it is a behavioral stress of the far greater significance of vegetable foods for the survival of these people.

By definition, the technotasks required the use of two or more subsistants and aids and thus were more complex than activities in which individual subsistants were used. Of the 12 Tiwi subsistants, only 6 were employed in associations. Thus, 50 percent of their survival technology was used singly to obtain foods. To measure the complexity of individual technotasks, the total number of subsistants and aids employed in each is counted. A glance at the Tiwi associations shows that the simplest involved food gathering, which was most often practiced and was most basic to the diet, while the most complex referred to hunting (bandicoot) that occurred rarely and was less significant for survival. Furthermore, of the total 12 associations, 58 percent concerned hunting and only 33 percent gathering. Thus, the Tiwi expended more efforts to obtain luxuries than their staple food. Given the richness of the environment, the Tiwi could adapt to it with minimum efforts and technological skills. Based on the detailed reports, I was able to identify six distinct microhabitats exploited by the Tiwi that are not labelled parallelly: the shore, the mangrove swamp, inland, a river, a hollow ground log, and a hollow tree branch. In general, the same number of microhabitats were exploited during the dry as the wet seasons. A greater diversity of food species was found inside hollow logs, where honey, bandicoots, and opossums could be obtained. Thus, in the sense of food variability, hollow logs appear to have provided the optimal microhabitat. On the other hand, during their inland trips, Tiwi women collected yams and cycad nuts which were the staple. In that sense, the inland portion of the islands offered the optimal habitat for survival. Thus, the Tiwi staples were obtained inland on an ongoing basis with a minimal subsistant inventory and minimal technological knowledge.

POINT BARROW ESKIMO

In striking contrast with the few and relatively simple forms made by the Tiwi, Eskimo material culture included a host of productions, many of which were extremely complex. The Tareumiut, or Point Barrow Eskimo of northern Alaska have been chosen to represent the technology of the ice-adapted northern hunters. The 1500 Tareumiut lived on Alaska's arctic coast. The residential and economic unit was the extended family, which moved over the tundra at different times during the year to exploit the diverse resources available, returning during the winter to the two major settlements of Point Barrow and Point Hope.

In a setting where survival depended largely on cooperation, the most adaptive social measures were those which extended a family's bonds. The Tareumiut maintained trading partnerships which had obvious economic advantages, and ensured distant sources of food, lodging, and sex, since partners also exchanged wives. Other extra-familial relationships were established between joking partners and between members of families joined by the adoption of children. The absence of social inequalities also serves to strengthen solidarity, and among the Tareumiut only a few captains of whaling boat crews, called *umialiks*, achieved a certain degree of authority through the accumulation of wealth. But status and wealth differences were quite unimportant as evidenced by the similar treatment of the dead. No funeral nor initiation ceremonies were performed and only one occasion, the Messenger Feast, was sufficiently elaborate to be considered a ceremony (Lantis 1947).

Technoeconomic Adaptation

Environmental limitations are often mentioned as causes for the unique material culture of the Eskimo. But in this study, the richness of the north Alaskan fauna and the habitat diversity are considered among the primary factors to have influenced the development of their structurally complex technology. The Tareumiut had a very diversified hunting economy and, unlike the other societies in this book, their associations were ordered into sea, land, and air hunting divisions.

Sea Mammal Hunting

baleen whale hunting: umiak/bailer/dog sled/ ice pick (whale spade)/meat (blubber) lure/*whale thrusting harpoon/whale lance*/flipper toggle line
beluga whale hunting: *whale-thrusting harpoon/whale lance*/flipper toggle line
walrus hunting: umiak/bailer/*toggle-headed walrus* (seal) *harpoon/whale lance*
open water seal hunting 1: umiak/bailer/*toggle-headed seal* (walrus) *harpoon/ hunting knife*
open water seal hunting 2: kayak/*seal dart and throwing board* (seal harpoon/ hunting knife (lance)/dog sled/blubber lure/drag
ice seal hunting: *toggle-headed seal* (walrus) *harpoon/long knife*/seal drag/dog sled/blubber lure
breathing-hole seal hunting: seal indicator/sealing stool (bearskin rug)/ caribou-skin cloak cover/*seal-thrusting harpoon*/seal drag/*hunting knife*/dog sled/ blubber lure
seal netting: ice pick/*seal net*/hooked-net setting pole/plummet line/snow wall/ seal-scratcher lure (ice pick, rattle) /*long knife*/seal drag/dog sled/blubber lure

The spring whaling season determined the economic activities of the rest of the year. A successful hunt yielded sufficient meat to free the settlement from food anxieties until the following year, but a poor hunt led to alternative, less productive sources. After the opening of leads in the ice, the men camped along the beach to await the migrating baleen whales. The hunters loaded their *umiak*, or large, open skin boat on a flat *dog sled* and transported it to the ice's edge on a path which had been previously cleared by hunters with *ice picks* or *spades*. The dog team was lured on with a piece of *meat* or *blubber* tied to a string and dragged in front of the dogs. About 15 umiaks were taken to sea, each with a captain or umialik, a harpooner, and several paddlers (Fig. 5). The *whale harpoon*, placed inside each boat, differed from others used by the Point Barrow Eskimo. The foreshaft, firmly tied to the shaft, did not loosen on impact and the head consisted of a walrus-ivory body, tipped with an arrow-shaped stone blade. A long seal-thong line passed through a hole in the head, was tied to the shaft, and held at its distal end two inflated sealskin floats (Fig. 6). An umiak was cautiously paddled near a great whale and the harpooner, standing on the bow, thrust the weapon deep into the mammal's back. As the whale sounded, the floats were thrown overboard. And the chase began. Before the wounded and frightened animal sur-

18   FORAGERS

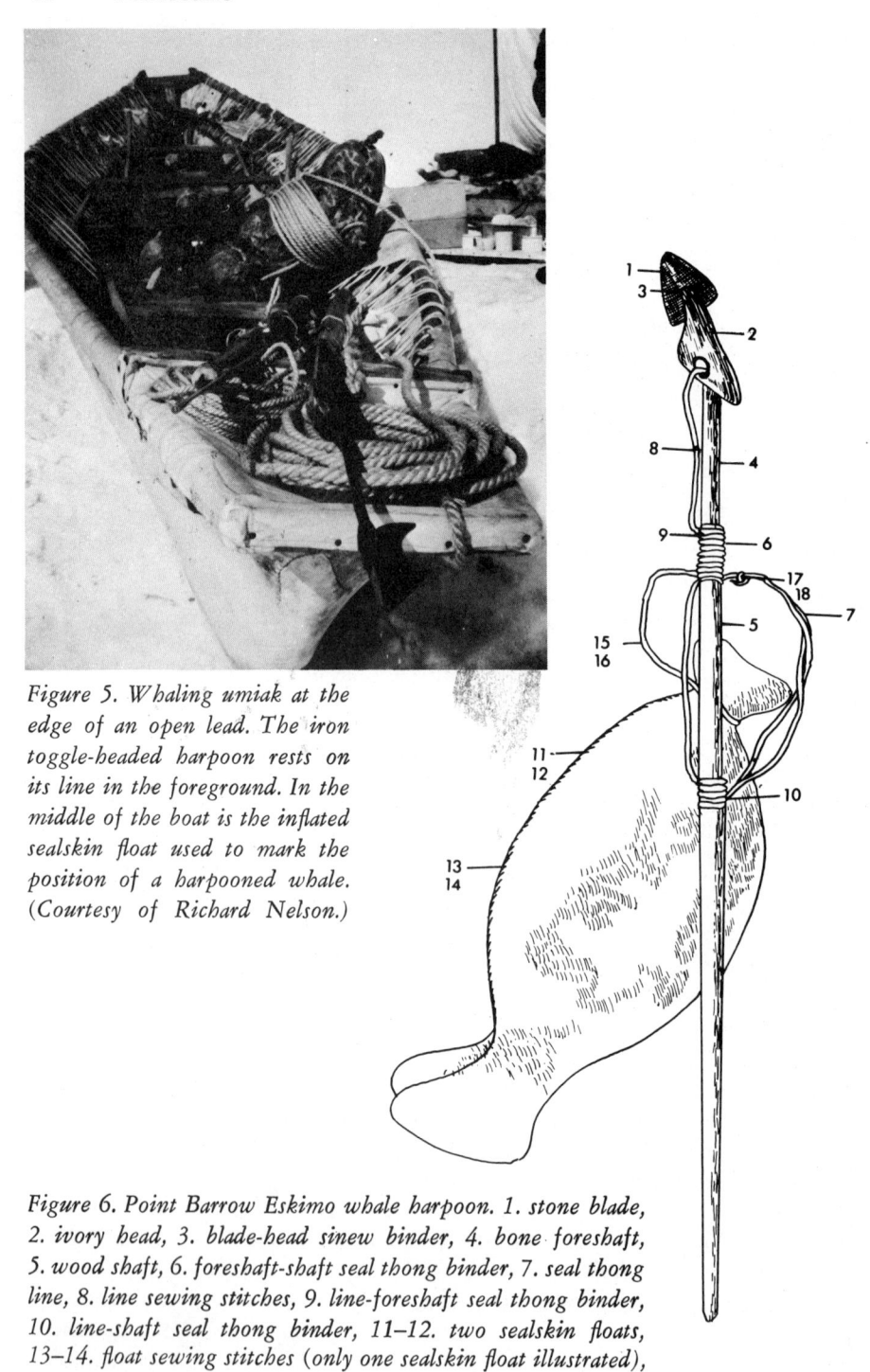

Figure 5. Whaling umiak at the edge of an open lead. The iron toggle-headed harpoon rests on its line in the foreground. In the middle of the boat is the inflated sealskin float used to mark the position of a harpooned whale. (Courtesy of Richard Nelson.)

Figure 6. Point Barrow Eskimo whale harpoon. 1. stone blade, 2. ivory head, 3. blade-head sinew binder, 4. bone foreshaft, 5. wood shaft, 6. foreshaft-shaft seal thong binder, 7. seal thong line, 8. line sewing stitches, 9. line-foreshaft seal thong binder, 10. line-shaft seal thong binder, 11–12. two sealskin floats, 13–14. float sewing stitches (only one sealskin float illustrated), 15–16. float-shaft seal thong lines, 17–18. line sewing stitches. (After Murdoch 1892.)

faced to breathe, the floats emerged to indicate where it would appear. Other harpoons were launched by as many crews as possible until the exhausted whale spouted blood, when it was killed with the flint-pointed *lances*. At the end of the hunt, the men attached a *toggled line* to the whale's flipper, by which they towed it ashore. Bowhead whales reappeared in the fall and were also harpooned in the open waters, although fewer animals were taken than in spring. One small whale species, the beluga, arrived in spring. They were harpooned from the ice edge since the Eskimo believed that they could hear the slightest sound in the water and would escape.

In midsummer, with the breakup of the ocean ice, walrus herds passed along the coast on ice floes. The men pursued the walrus in *umiaks*, captured them with *toggle-headed seal harpoons*, and killed them with *lances*. The seal and walrus harpoon was the most complex subsistant manufactured by the Tareumiut. The head consisted of a slate blade inserted in an ivory piece which detached from the heavy ivory foreshaft and toggled inside a stricken animal. The head was connected by a short baleen strip to the main line, held by an ivory peg to the long spruce shaft. A finger rest, also fastened to the shaft, enabled the harpooner to manipulate the weapon. An inflated sealskin float attached to the main line with sinew served to tag a walrus until the hunters approached it. Walrus were hunted until the end of August, when many families travelled east to exchange oil and blubber for the caribou, fox, and wolverine skins of other Eskimo and Indians.

Seal hunting was less exciting than whale or walrus hunting but more important in terms of subsistence, since seals were the most widely distributed, abundant, and reliable species. While waiting at the edge of the ice for whales to appear, the male crews were on the lookout for harbor and bearded seals that were *harpooned* from the *umiaks*, and killed with *knives*. During the fall whaling trips, seals were also hunted from *kayaks*. A set of three *darts* was propelled in succession with a *throwing board*. Each dart consisted of a spruce shaft with an attached ivory socketpiece that served to improve its accuracy. A line connected the detachable head, a flat, barbed bone point, to the socketpiece and a separate extension bound the head to the shaft. The seal was killed with a *knife* and dragged home by a woman who attached the animal to a *sled* with a *seal thong*.

During the summer, about one fourth of the population remained near the village to hunt ringed and bearded seals sleeping on top of the ice. A large number of these animals could be obtained with *toggle-headed harpoons*. A different seal hunting method was to mark a seal's breathing hole or an ice crack with a slender *ivory rod* topped with feathers which served to indicate the presence of a seal. The hunter sat on a *stool* or a *polar-bear skin* and covered himself with a caribouskin *cloak* until an animal appeared. A different, less complex *harpoon* was used than on other occasions. A short shaft was tied to a long foreshaft, and an ice pick attached at the end served on occasion to test the thin ice over which the hunter walked. The most productive sealing method was to set a large meshed baleen *net* parallel to the shore in summer and under the ice or across lagoons or stream mouths in winter. One hundred seals were reportedly netted in a single day at Point Barrow. With the aid of a long *hooked pole*, a hunter inserted the net attached to a *line* through one of three small holes chipped in the ice. A second line, fastening the other corner of the net, stretched it under the ice like a curtain. At night, the men sat behind low *snow walls* to protect themselves from the wind and lured the seals, scratching the ice with *seal-claw scratchers, picks,* or *rattles* made by hanging pendants on a piece of wood. Since the nets only entangled the seals, they must have been killed with *knives*. When the women felt like it, they drove to the nets with their *dog sleds* and carried the catch back to the village.

Land Mammal Hunting

swimming caribou hunting: kayak/*lance*
summer caribou hunting: *caribou guides/bow and arrows*/bow wrist guard/quiver/ bow case
fall caribou hunting: *bow and arrows*/bow wrist guard/quiver/bow case/snowshoes
spring caribou hunting: dog sled/blubber lure/*bow and arrows*/bow wrist guard/ quiver/bow case
caribou trapping: *pitfall/lance*
polar bear hunting: dog sled/blubber lure/blubber decoy/*bow and arrows*/bow wrist guard/quiver/bow case

---

caribou snare
fox deadfall

    Less predictable than the sea mammal movements were the caribou migrations, and their contribution to the food supply was considerably smaller. During the summer, *kayakers lanced* caribou swimming in rivers, but more commonly entire families travelled to the coast. There they set up a *line of posts* to guide the herds towards the beach, where they were pursued and killed with *bows and arrows*. The Tareumiut manufactured a composite bow consisting of separate antler pieces attached to a spruce shaft and reinforced with a sinew backing to increase the weapon's elasticity. To protect their skin, the hunters tied a piece of *antler* on their *wrist*. The spruce arrows were unique since the point was attached to the shaft by a sinew line that did not loosen on impact. A *quiver* and sealskin *bow case* were sewn side-by-side and were usually carried slung across the back.

    In the fall, a few families remained inland to hunt, with *bows and arrows*, the caribou that were migrating south. The ice conditions required the use of *snowshoes*. More caribou were hunted during the spring migrations, when the men pursued the herds on *dog sleds*. After a snowstorm, caribou were trapped in snow covered *pitfalls*, baited with reindeer moss and grass, that were dug along stream or lake banks. Presumably the captured animals were killed with *lances*. Caribou were also taken with rawhide *snares*, spread with sticks across an animal's path. The men pursued polar bear on the winter ice with their *sleds* and lured the animals within arrow range with *blubber* or *meat*. A fox was trapped in a *deadfall* consisting of a small ice mound inside which was a meat or blubber bait. The entrance was spanned by a heavy log supported on two upright sticks. When a fox moved the trigger, the log fell on the animal.

Bird Hunting

duck hunting: *guide posts*/gravel pits/*bow and arrow* (bolas)/bow wrist guard/
 quiver/bow case
duck hunting 2: stool/*bolas* (bow and arrows)
duck hunting: *bird dart and throwing board* (spear)/umiak (kayak)/bailer

---

snare
gorge

Some families moved to the coast in spring to hunt the large flocks of migrating ducks and geese. The men raised a *line of posts* along the bend of the beach and concealed themselves in shallow *pits*. When the birds flew by, the hunters left their hiding places, sometimes gathering hundreds in a week with *bows and arrows* or *bolas*. Women and children, who commonly hunted birds with bolas, carried a set in a pouch around the neck. Each set consisted of walrus-ivory balls, attached by braided sinew lines to a feather handle (Fig. 7). The hunters also used *bolas* to capture the ducks that flew by when they were seal hunting on the ice, and with *bird darts* and *throwing boards* they shot ducks from their *umiaks* or *kayaks*. The most complex bird dart had two terminal ivory prongs and three curved prongs medially placed on the shaft (Fig. 8). Ptarmigan, a nonmigratory land-bird species, was caught with baleen *snares* attached to the ground on the birds' paths with wood stakes. Gulls and arctic terns could be obtained with *gorges*, manufactured by coating with blubber pieces of baleen that were tied to wood pegs with strings. The pegs were concealed by covering them with snow, and when a bird swallowed the blubber coating and attempted to fly away, the attachment prevented its escape and the baleen killed it.

Fishing

shoal-water fishing: *gill net*/kayak
tidal-stream fishing 1: *dam/leister*
tidal-stream fishing 2: *set bag net/dam*
ice fishing: ice pick/baleen scoop/*fishhook assembly*

Most fishing took place during the summer when the men set baleen *gill nets* at right angles to the beach from their *kayaks*. Every few days, they checked these nets for whitefish, salmon, and trout. In shallow water, where a net could not be set, the men built a *dam*, presumably of rocks, and speared fish with *leisters*, a weapon provided with a short, medial piercing prong and two external ones to which two short bone barbs were attached. The women were in charge of collecting the fish caught inside conical *sinew traps*, (*set bag nets*), set permanently in streams along the coast close to a *dam*. Women also fished through the ice in winter, chopping holes with *ice picks* and gathering the fragments with baleen *scoops* or *dippers*, which consisted of two antler pieces mounted on a handle. The *fishing assembly* included a long baleen line bound to a spruce rod and a shorter strip that joined an ivory sinker to a pair of lures with two copper hooks attached. The main catch was tomcod, but polar cod and sculpin were also taken, and with

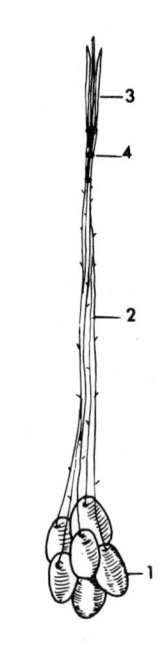

Figure 7. Point Barrow Eskimo bolas. 1. ivory balls, 2. attachment braided sinew lines, 3. feather vane handle, 4. line-handle sinew binder. (After Murdoch 1892.)

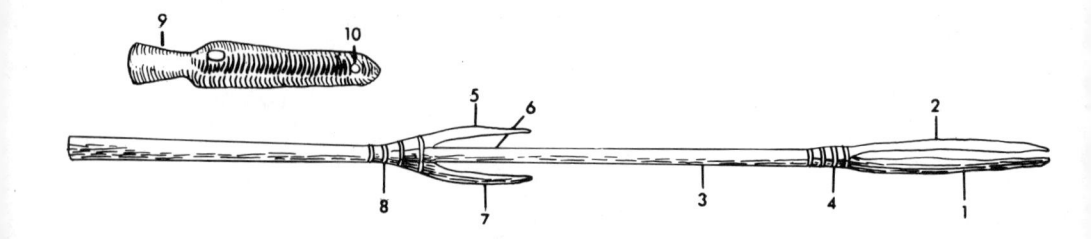

Figure 8. Point Barrow Eskimo bird dart and spear thrower. 1–2. ivory end prongs, 3. spruce shaft, 4. prong-shaft sinew binder, 5–7. ivory side prongs, 8. side prongs–shaft sinew binder, 9. spruce throwing board, 10. ivory peg. (After Murdoch 1892.)

a baited hook they fished burbot. In deep rivers, using a rod and hooked line, the women fished for trout, grayling, and smelt.

Storants

During the winter, after a caribou slaughtering session, the meat that could not be consumed or carried back to the village was buried under the snow and the place marked with slender ivory rods with attached feathers. In summer, a storage pit was dug in the gravel, close to the camp, to keep the excess seal meat until the winter. A large bin framed with whale's ribs and placed at the entrance of a winter house served to keep tons of blubber and whale, seal, caribou, fish, and duck meat. The Tareumiut also stored meat in structures similar to the compartment built on one side of the entrance passage of a house. Here, the men brought the meat from more permanent storants and set it on racks to thaw out. Near each winter house stood one or more small, underground, blubber-storing cellar roofed with whales' bones, and in the fall the men built many small, snow storehouses where diverse foods were stored for a long time. Inside the house, the Tareumiut kept a spruce or fir bucket filled with water from a pond or lake. Blubber and meat were also stored in these receptacles. During the winter, they placed a large tub in the house to catch the water melting from a snow lump set on a wall rack next to a lamp. And on hunting trips, the women carried snow-filled sealskin canteens inside their parkas to melt the snow with the heat of their bodies. In similar seal containers they also stored oil.

Analysis

Unlike the Tiwi, the Point Barrow Eskimo lacked natural subsistants and the instruments usually used to gather plants, presumably because of the scarcity of economically productive vegetable foods. The Eskimo did, however, manufacture subsistants representing the major classes, including complex forms and facilities that were not found among the Tiwi.[2]

It was suggested above that the Tiwi may have lacked complex weapons because they were usually employed by males and the culture stressed collecting vegetable foods by the females. The Eskimo subsistants could also be divided according to the sex employing them. Except for the complex bolas, females used only simple facilities. Men, on the other hand, utilized predominantly both simple and complex weapons and a few facilities. In the sense that facilities were subsistants that received incoming prey, they resembled the containers usually employed by the women to cook or carry food and water. One reason why women most often used facilities may have been their greater familiarity with containers.

A more accurate measure of the structural complexity of a society's equipment than the total number of types is obtained with component numbers. The 20 Point Barrow Eskimo subsistants were made with 133 components. This figure differs strikingly from the Tiwi equivalent of 15. The most complex Tareumiut subsistant,

---

[2] Subsistant and storant tables are near the end of each chapter.

TABLE 3. TIWI AND POINT BARROW ESKIMO SUBSISTANTS

	Tiwi	Point Barrow Eskimo
Naturefact		
implement		
instrument		
simple	crab-pulling stick(1)* honey-removal stick(1) collecting stone(1)	
weapon		
simple	stone missile(1) club(1) missile stick(1)	
Artifact		
implement		
instrument		
simple	honey-removal stick(1) digging stick(1) ax(4)	
weapon		
simple	throwing stick(1) club(1) spear(1)	hunting knife (4) (1 var.**) whale lance (4) (2 var.)
complex		leister(10) bird dart & throwing board (10) (1 var.) bow & arrow (16) (2 var.) seal dart & throwing board(17) toggle-headed seal harpoon (28) (4 var.)
facility		
tended		
simple		dam(1) caribou guides(1) bird snare(2) duck guide posts (3) caribou snare(3) seal net(4) fishhook assembly(8) (4 var.)
complex		caribou pitfall(3) bolas(4)
untended		
simple		set bag net(2) gill net(3) gorge (5) (1 var.)
complex		fox deadfall(5)

* The numbers between parentheses are the components of each subsistant.
** Variety.

TABLE 4. TIWI AND POINT BARROW ESKIMO STORANTS

	Tiwi	Point Barrow Eskimo
Naturefact		
receptacle		
short-term		snow pit(1)
long-term		gravel pit(1)
structure		
short-term	turtle-egg sand deposit(1)	
	tree-honey deposit(1)	
Artifact		
receptacle		
short-term	basket(6)	bucket(6)
		tub(6)
long-term		storage bin(2)
		sealskin canteen(3)
structure		
short-term	swamp-yam bed(2)	winter house room(3)
	cycad-nut recipient(2)	
	yam-branch covering(2)	
long-term		storehouse(2)
		whalebone cellar(4)

the toggle-headed harpoon used to hunt seals and walrus, had 28 parts. Perhaps the greater component complexity of implements (89) compared to facilities (44) may be explained by the numerous components making up the harpoon. Murdoch, in opposition to other authors, stressed that seals, rather than whales or walrus, were the staple Tareumiut food. His view is supported by the greater number of diverse subsistants used to take seals, by contrast with the single whale-taking weapon. The extreme development of the sealing harpoon is additional evidence that seals did represent a most significant portion of the Tareumiut diet.

Unlike the Tiwi, the Eskimo did not use any multipurpose forms, but formal variation flourished with a diversity of arrows, darts, fishhooks, harpoons, and lances. Since Eskimo subsistants filled all the taxa in the classification except the simplest, that is naturefacts and instruments, these people may be presumed to have mastered all the functional possibilities encompassed by the taxonomy. The functional categories ordered from the simplest to the most complex comprised forms employed hand held (a knife), anatomically projected (a lance, leister, harpoon), materially projected (bird dart and seal dart with throwing board, bow and arrow), attended self-acting (dam, bird and caribou snare, seal net, caribou pitfall), and unattended self-acting (gill net, set bag net, gorge, deadfall). A gradual increase in technological sophistication characterizes these functional classes corresponding to the structural categories of the taxonomy. The hand-held forms required greater human expenditures in their use than the unattended self-acting, which functioned alone. Yet, by contrast, greater efforts must have been expended to manufacture the unattended sets than the hand-held implements, although this expenditure occurred only once. The resultant subsistant worked in the hunter's absence an unspecified number of times, while leaving him free to pursue other activities. Presumably, very advanced foragers would have had more untended facilities than any other subsistant class. That the Tareumiut had only four suggests that more complex survival inventories existed, as was the case exemplified by the seven Nabesna untended sets and the eight possessed by the Caribou Eskimo (Oswalt 1973:149).

The Point Barrow Eskimo storants included all technological possibilities such as natural and artifactual forms, tight receptacles, and loosely containing structures for long- or short-term use, implying that the storing technology was well developed. The Eskimo long-term storage devices and facilities had a common conceptual basis since both required the capacity to wait and the expectation of future returns. In contrast, the Tiwi had neither long-term storants nor facilities.

Sixteen of the 20 total Tareumiut subsistants were used in association. Since the associations represented the most complex tasks, the technological involvement of their economic pursuits was great. One basic assumption of this approach to technoeconomic activities is to regard the relative increase in parts as representing greater complexity. In this context, seal netting was the most complex activity, since it required the use of 10 forms. Counting all the subsistant associations, the Tareumiut had 21, of which 38 percent referred to sea mammal hunting, 28 percent to land mammal hunting, 19 percent to fishing, and the rest to bird hunting. Undoubtedly, a greater strategic diversity was required to obtain the sea dwelling animals than any other food source.

The habitats exploited by the Tareumiut included the sea, over the ice, under the ice, the coast, a river, and on the snow. The sea was the optimal setting for Tarumiut survival, for here the greatest diversity of animals was obtained, including walrus, whales, fish, ducks, and the seal staple. A comparison of the habitat information with the species availability and the subsistant data, indicates that the Tareumiut used more facilities beneath the ice to obtain seals and fish than implements in the sea to obtain sea mammals. Thus, more energy was expended by these people to manufacture the sealing equipment and more different ways were employed to take seals that any other animal. The causes may have been partly environmental, for seals were not only more reliable than whales or caribou, but they could be hunted the year round. Whales were mainly hunted in spring and their migrations were not too predictable, while caribou, irregularly hunted throughout the year, were the least predictable of all species hunted by the Tareumiut. Thus, both Eskimo and Tiwi depended primarily on the food resource that was available the year round, and while the Tiwi adapted to their surroundings with the simplest of technologies, the Tareumiut did so with highly complex manufactures. This dichotomous situation is observed in their subsistants, which are represented by exclusive categories except for the simple weapon class that was present in both (Table 3).

HOW TO USE THE SUBSISTANT TAXONOMY AND THE TECHNOTASK APPROACH TO MATERIAL CULTURE

In order to analyze the survival strategies of any people, the following questions should be answered. Each set of 11 questions serves to complete one row in the accompanying chart (Table 5, p. 28). In other words, each set of answers will refer to one task at a time. If two or more subsistants and/or aids are used in one task, identify all in the blank space next to the question.

1. What is the subsistence *activity*? _____
2. Within the activity, what *task* is performed with material forms? _____
3. What *subsistant* is used in the task? _____
4. If the subsistant is an *implement*, is it an *instrument* or a *weapon*? ____
5. Is the instrument or weapon *simple* or *complex*? _____
6. How many *components* does it have? _____
7. If the subsistant is a facility, is it a *tended set* or an *untended set*? ____
8. Is the tended or untended set *simple* or *complex*? _____
9. How many *components* does it have? _____
10. What *aid* is used in association with the subsistant? _____
11. Is the aid *natural* or *artifactual*? _____

To organize the information, identify each row in Table 5 with a Roman numeral, as in the example, and complete the answers to the 11 questions in columns (below). The data, which comes from the Tiwi gathering technotasks, is also used to illustrate the chart.

Question	I	II	III	IV
1	gathering	gathering	gathering	gathering
2	plants	shellfish	honey	turtle eggs
3	digging stick	collecting stone	honey removal stick	—
4	instrument	instrument	instrument	—
5	simple	simple	simple	—
6	one	one	one	—
7	—	—	—	—
8	—	—	—	—
9	—	—	—	—
10	hands	hands	ladder ax	hands turtle-egg probe
11	natural	natural	artifactual artifactual	natural artifactual

Next, place the answers to the eleven questions in the appropriate spaces in the chart. The number of components should be placed next to each subsistant, in parentheses. After repeating the procedure for two or more people, compare:

(a) the relative number of implements and facilities
(b) the relative number of instruments and weapons
(c) the relative number of tended and untended sets
(d) the total number of simple and complex subsistants
(e) the number of simple and complex forms in each class
(f) the total component numbers by class
(g) the total number of subsistants and aids in each association
(h) the total number of associations in each activity

TABLE 5. COMPREHENSIVE CHART OF THE UNITS OF ANALYSIS

ACTIVITY	TECHNOTASK		ASSOCIATION							
	Task		Subsistant						Aid	
			Implement				Facility			
			instrument		weapon		tended		untended		natural	artifactual
			simple	complex	simple	complex	simple	complex	simple	complex		
Gathering	I plant gathering	digging stick (1)									
	II shellfish gathering	collecting stone (1)								hands	
	III honey gathering	honey removal stick (1)								hands	ladder ax
	IV turtle egg gathering									hands	turtle-egg probe

Hunting	V	turtle, etc. hunting	spear (1)		canoe bailer
	VI	joint wallaby hunt	spear (1)	fire	beater sticks
	VII	bandicoot hunting	club (1)	dog hands	tree probe ax
	VIII	opossum hunting 1	club (1)	fire	
	IX	opossum hunting 2	club (1)		sticks stones
	X	opossum hunting 3		hands	ladder tree probe
	XI	opossum hunting 4	club (1)		ladder probe ax
Fishing	XII	mangrove fishing	spear (1)		canoe bailer

CASE STUDY INTERACTIONS

1. Closely following the classificatory guidelines introduced for the subsistants, devise a similar taxonomy for one nonsubsistant class, utilizing the data from *The Two Worlds of the Washo* (Downs 1966), or from any ethnography of your choice.

   What generalizations can you make on the basis of your classification that will help to explain further:

   (a) the technology of the society from which you obtained your data
   (b) the economy of your chosen group
   (c) the technological adaptation of the culture under consideration, to its environment, or the environmental restraints on the material culture

EXAMPLE:

CLASSIFICATION OF SOME TIWI CONTAINERS

	Naturefact	*Artifact*
Storing	honey mark (1)	food basket (7)
Carrying	pandanus strip (1)	palm-leaf water container (3)
Eating or Drinking	mollusk-shell cup (1)	paperbark water cup (2)

   (a) In evolutionary terms, eating or drinking receptacles probably preceded both carrying receptacles and the storing containers which were considered in this book. This deduction follows from the study's assumption that increasing component numbers indicate an increase in structural complexity.

2. Devise a model for the effects of acculturation on the subsistants and technotasks of a hunting people. Consider what happened to the Tareumiut subsistant inventory when the rifle was introduced. And the technotask variability? Case Studies that are useful in this context include *The Two Worlds of the Washo* (Downs 1966) and *A Kwakiutl Village and School* (Wolcott 1967).

3. Using either the materials in this book, or *The Cheyennes: Indians of the Great Plains* (Hoebel 1960) and *The Semai: A Nonviolent People of Malaya* (Dentan 1968), test with the subsistant taxonomy the two following hypotheses:

   (a) that there is a direct correlation between facilities and great caloric amounts harvested, and an indirect relationship between implements and great caloric amounts
   (b) that more food may be procured with complex subsistants than with the simpler forms.

Postulate alternative hypotheses.

3
Pastoralists[1]

PASTORAL TIBETANS

Historical circumstances have hindered the collection of information on the aboriginal Tibetan nomads. Fortunately, because of two outstanding descriptions of the black-tent pastoralists inhabiting the northeastern province of Amdo, it is possible to reconstruct the aboriginal culture. In Tibet, altitude determined the ecological boundaries of the aBrog pastoralists who lived in a high, discontinuous area that included open steppelands, deep valleys, river banks, and mountain slopes, characterized by diurnal and seasonal climatic extremes. To withstand the diurnal temperature variations, the nomads needed special clothing. The typical dress was a sheepskin coat with long sleeves and a high collar. Clothing details as well as hair styles varied with the tribe, and all men characteristically rubbed their hair with butter in order to repel the abundant insects.

The extended family lived in a tent made from black yak hair. These rectangular structures, with flat roofs suspended by ropes tied to external poles, resembled giant spiders. The camp size was determined by the number of domesticated animals and the quality of the grasslands. Occasionally, a family with a large number of animals camped alone, but sometimes 20 to 30 tents made up a settlement. The original Tibetans believed in nature demons and spirits of the dead. Buddhism, introduced into Tibet in the seventh century A.D., resulted in a unique mixture of magic and mysticism. Its adoption partially conflicted with the native culture which had previously stressed the hunting of wild game next to the domestication of herds.

Technoeconomic Adaptation

Besides raising animals and hunting wild game, the aboriginal Tibetans made yearly trading expeditions to the deep valleys, where they exchanged the meat and skins of their herds for the cereal and brick tea of the farmers. This custom was apparently very old, for at the time of historical contact, brick tea and tsamba, a parched barley flour, were staples along with butter. Although the Tibetans have used money for a long time, brick tea was the preferred unit of value.

---

[1] The technological information on the Pastoral Tibetans was primarily obtained from Hermanns (1949) and Rockhill (1895). Bogoras' (1904–1909) outstanding description on the Chukchi was the sole source on their technology and subsistence activities.

When attempting to identify the herders' tasks as discrete phenomena, as with the Tiwi and Eskimo, it became apparent that each pastoralist task was a step in a series whose ultimate objective was the consumption of the herds. This differed from seal netting, caribou trapping, or fishing, for each of these foraging tasks fulfilled the ultimate aim without intervening activities. In other words, certain tasks were required to tend the domestic herds in addition to those required to hunt or gather wild foods. Consequently, the pastoralist technotasks were treated differently than those of foragers, and each was identified by its ultimate purpose, such as controlling the herd size, training the herds, and protecting them.

Animal Husbandry

Animal Maintenance
  Regulating Herd Size
    moving herds: pack saddle/riding saddle/whip/*sling*/life vest/skin raft
    haying: plow/yoke/leading rope/*sickle*
    gelding: *hobble*/gelding sinew (knife)/searing rod
    branding sheep and yak: *hobble*/knife
    branding horses: *hobble*/fire brand
  Training Herds
    breaking horses: rope/bridle/riding saddle/whip
  Protecting Herds
    rounding up sheep: riding saddle/whip/*sling*/dog
    killing predators: riding saddle/whip/*spear*
    confining sheep: folds
    confining horses: *fetters/stall*
    confining yak: *hobble/cattle pen*
Food Harvest
    animal slaughter: *hobble/slaughtering rope* (knife)
    blood tapping: *hobble/knife*
    milking: *cow tether/calf tether*/calf-skin decoy/*milking hook and pail*/girdle

Since Tibet is the only place in the world where wild yak are found, it is seemingly conclusive that the yak was domesticated in that plateau. Although less numerous than sheep, yak were the main Tibetan domesticates, for they provided most necessities such as food, transportation, and usable raw materials. The domestic yaks, slightly smaller than their wild counterparts, had long, curved, pointed horns, and most were black. The common cattle introduced into Tibet from China were not raised in the high regions of the Tibetan plateau except for an occasional bull that hybridized with yaks to produce a hardier breed of cattle.

A main concern of all herders was to keep the size of the stocks at an optimum level. If the herds decreased in numbers famine might follow, but if they were allowed to increase unchecked the pasturelands would be overgrazed and unnecessary stock death would result. To avoid both disasters, the nomads had to keep their flocks within optimal limits. The most essential task was to feed the herds, usually accomplished by merely moving the animals to fresh pastures. The Tibetans generally moved from three to eight times a year. They transported most belongings on yaks, and in fast trips horses were also used. A typical *pack saddle* consisted of an arched wood tree, placed on top of felt pads, and a blanket with leather straps to tie the load; a saddle girth and broad, wool breast straps com-

Figure 9. Loaded Tibetan yak. (Courtesy of the Smithsonian Institution National Anthropological Archives.)

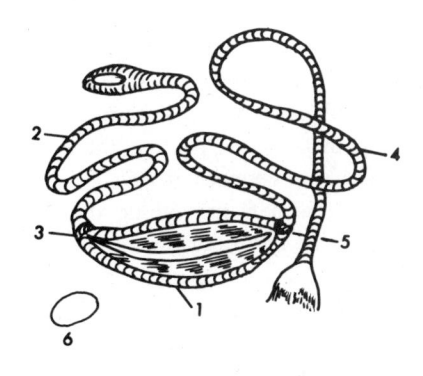

Figure 10. Pastoral Tibetan sling. 1. wool hair strap, 2. holding string, 3. strap-string sewing stitches, 4. leash, 5. strap-leash sewing stitches, 6. missile stone. (After Rockhill 1894.)

pleted the equipment (Fig. 9). *Whips* were made by attaching leather lashes to short handles. The *riding saddles* used on yak or horses had more elements than their pack counterpart. More felt pads were used over and under the seat, and additional components included a leather harness, stirrups, a hind girth, and a long rawhide rope extending from the saddle to the bit, which consisted of a large ring connected to the headstall and reins.

The *sling* was the typical weapon and it was carried, by both men and women, hanging from their belts (Fig. 10). Two strings were fastened on each side of a leather pocket, one furnished with an eye for the passage of the thumb and the other braided into a leash to serve as a whip. To cross a river, a man placed his clothes inside an *inflated sheep's skin* and lay on top of it. However, most people and cargo crossed rivers on *skin rafts* made by stretching inflated sheep or yak's skins over wood frames. A single raft accommodated two to three persons and 200 pounds of cargo. During the summer, the herders migrated to the higher ranges, and in the fall they moved to their lower, winter quarters to begin haying for the winter months. It is not known whether the original Tibetans knew how to make hay but apparently the plow, a cultivating aid, was introduced into Tibet from China in the second century A.D. To prepare the ground, the men tied the slightly curved wood *plow* without a share to a *yoke* placed about an oxen's neck. One man led the animal by a *rope* and another guided the plow. When the planted grasses were ripe, they were harvested with iron-bladed *sickles* and fed to the herds.

In order to regulate herd size, the Tibetans gelded male yaks before they were a year old. The animals were held with *ropes* and castrated with strong *sinew threads* tightened around the testicles to prevent the blood from circulating. In pre-Buddhist times, this operation was performed with *knives* and the cut seared with hot *metal rods*. Presumably, the same methods were employed to geld rams and stallions. In a sense, animal branding also served to regulate numbers, since herds were identified by that means. A herder cut a notch on the left ear of a sheep or cattle with a *knife*, and horses captured from wild herds were marked with fire-heated *irons* on their left legs. The only Tibetan domesticates that were reportedly trained were horses. To break a colt, an unmounted horseman attached *ropes* to both rings of the *snaffle bit* and pulled them from side to side until the animal allowed a rider to mount it, bareback first, and later with a *saddle*.

Sheep were more difficult to keep than yaks, since they were watered every second day and, unlike the other stock, they dispersed easily and became prey to wolves. To guard the flocks which provided food and clothing, each shepherd carried a *sling* and was aided by 2 to 12 fierce *dogs*. The shepherds often tracked down wolves on horseback and killed them with their *spears*. At night they kept sheep near their camps (Fig. 11), and the lambs were confined to *folds* or portable corrals, made of boards and poles, to prevent them from milking the ewes. Horses were hobbled at night with *fetters* fashioned by tying rawhide and sheep's-wool thongs with wood toggles. Since the mares and colts remained by the stallions, they did not need to be hobbled. During winter nights, the horses were confined inside stone-walled *courtyards* and tethered beneath the houses' roofs. The yaks were *tethered* inside stone *enclosures* built next to the houses. The least economically significant animal, because it had inferior meat and hair, was the goat, which also required the least care.

The bulk of the nomads' diet consisted of yak and sheep flesh processed by the men. A common slaughtering method was to strangle the bound animals with *thin ropes*. However, before the introduction of Buddhism into Tibet, *knives* were used for this purpose. After *hobbling* oxen and barren female yaks, the herdsmen obtained blood from the animals' neck and shoulder vessels with *knives*. Coagulated blood mixed with cheese was considered a delicacy. Blood was also prepared as sausages, together with flesh and fat, placed inside cleaned guts.

Three activities were performed throughout the year: collecting dung and preparing it for fuel, travelling to trade centers, and milking the ewes. Yak milk was considered the best; sheep milk was inferior in quality, and mares were never milked. The women milked yak cows in the morning and at night, after tying them head to head by means of a *rope* through their nose rings and attached to

Figure 11. Nomadic Tibetan camp. Pastoral Tibetan camp, with sheep and yak herds in the background, and a black tent in the middle of the photograph. (Courtesy of the Smithsonian Institution National Anthropological Archives.)

a *long line* extended between two *posts*. The calves were similarly tied with *neck ropes* to an extended *line* to prevent them from nursing. If a calf died, a woman struck the cow's udder with the dead animal's grass-filled *skin* to deceive it into releasing its milk. The liquid was received in a *wood pail* suspended from the woman's *belt* by means of a double brass hook. The milk derivatives processed by the women included butter, cheese, yogurt, buttermilk, and whey. The milk was processed inside a churn, a long, leather bag which was either rolled on the ground or suspended on a moving animal to initiate the curdling. Butter, besides being a staple food, was a weight measure, a tanning agent for animal skins, a cosmetic against sun and wind, and a hair dressing. The Tibetans did not know how to make real cheese, but a white substance was prepared by heating the buttermilk in a copper kettle over a dry dung fire; the whey ran off when the nutrient was placed inside a leather bag and the white "cheese" remained. To make yogurt, the Tibetans left residues of previously-processed milk in pails to accelerate the acid forming process when fresh milk was added.

Hunting

wild animal hunting: riding saddle/whip/*bow and arrow* (spear)
trapping: *game trap/spear* (sword)

Because the domestic herds had to be kept within certain numerical limits, supplementary proteins were obtained by hunting. But the introduction of Buddhism into Tibet ended this activity through the prohibition to spill blood. The following information is not considered as complete as the other economic data due to the late date of the ethnographies.

In prehistoric times, during their spring moves, the mounted herders hunted wild animals with *bows and arrows*. Wild yak, sheep, antelope, gazelle, and especially musk deer were commonly hunted game. The native bow consisted of a simple birch staff with a sinew string, and an arrow with a stone point and three feathers. Hermanns (1949) believed the bow and arrow to have been aboriginal, but Rockhill (1895) considered it of Chinese origin. In pre-Chinese times the nomads also trapped game. The *trapping device* consisted of a rope ring with sharp-pointed slips of wood attached to the inner surface converging towards the center, where a gap remained to hold the animal's foot. The trap, set in a small hole near a watering place, was covered with earth and attached to the ground by ropes. The concealed hunter killed a trapped animal with a *spear* that had a narrow, two-edged iron blade tied to a long shaft with an iron coil wound around its length, and a heavy iron shoe attached at its distal end (Fig. 12).

Vegetable foods were seldom eaten. In the fall, a herdswoman gathered various species of mushrooms and in spring she harvested a few varieties of tubers with a *hoe* which had a long, slightly-curved handle and an attached, pointed, wood blade.

Storants

Given their nomadic existence and the nature of their food resources, the Tibetans possessed several storage devices. Butter, the staple, was stored either in goatskins, yak-hair cloth, or wood boxes. Butter and tsampa were also stored in leather bags; sour milk was kept inside wood tubs for long periods, and yaks' stomachs served to store water. The tent was the only structural storant, in which cheese and meat strips were hung from the roof ropes and all other storing containers were kept on the walls.

Analysis

The increased human control over the natural resources is usually considered to have preceded the proliferation and development of material forms. Thus, herders and farmers who learned to tend and cultivate food species should have more complex extractive technologies than foragers. A tentative assessment will be offered in the last chapter, where all the information will be compared. In the meantime, it is notable that the total number of Tibetan subsistants was merely 16, of which 12 were employed in animal husbandry activities and the remainder used to obtain wild game. Yet, it should be emphasized that data about foraging is not considered to be very accurate. One obvious difference between the subsistants of herders and hunters is the multiplication of restraining facilities among herders. The Tibetans posssesed nine facilities, of which seven were used to hold or confine the stocks.

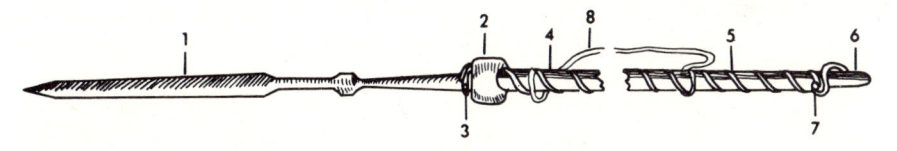

Figure 12. Pastoral Tibetan spear. 1. iron point, 2. iron support, 3. nail, 4. wood shaft, 5. coiled-iron band, 6. iron shoeing, 7. nail, 8. leather binder. (After Rockhill 1894.)

In relative terms, the Tibetan subsistants had very few components, since the total number was 63. Despite the predominance of herding activities, the most complex subsistants were those employed to hunt: a bow and arrow with nine components and a spear with eight. Thus, a greater technological expenditure was required to make the foraging implements than the herding ones, which is logically sound if one realizes that the harder the task at hand the more complex the technology. The domesticated animals were readily available and most tending facilities merely confined the stocks.

The Tibetans had 15 survival strategies and 86 percent centered on animal husbandry, whereas only 13 percent were dedicated to hunting. The reader must remember that only those tasks performed with two or more forms are considered to be technotasks. Likewise, the movement of the herds to other pastures represented the association which required the greatest number of technological forms (six). I noted above that the most complex subsistants were used in hunting. The fact that the most involved associations referred to animal husbandry suggests that the associations or technotasks might be a better index of the economic focus of a culture than the subsistants.

Food storage becomes important under a variety of circumstances, such as the seasonality of the resources, their nature, the prevalent climate, or the mobility patterns of the people under consideration. For the pastoral Tibetans, storage was significant because of their constant moves and because their stock was not immediately available for consumption. Storants used to keep one kind of food will be considered to be specialized, and those which store two or more edibles will be called generalized, or diversified. The Tibetans kept butter, their staple, either in a goatskin, a yak-hair cloth, or a wood box. Two other specialized storants were the wood tubs in which sour milk was stored and the yak stomachs used to contain water. Only two diversified storants were used: the leather bags to store butter and tsampa, and the tents in which all foods were kept. Thus, a greater diversity of forms was used to store the staple than any other food. Furthermore, storage among these herders was predominantly specialized since, of the seven storant types, five were specialized and two diversified. In terms of components, a dichotomy was found between short- and long-term storants. Short-term receptacles possessed from one to three components whereas long term storants had from two to seventeen components. These almost complementary ranges suggest that the component numbers are indexes to storant usage. Those forms that preserved food for long periods seemingly had more components than those which were only temporarily employed.

REINDEER CHUKCHI

Bogoras, who wrote the definitive work on the Chukchi (1904–1909), considered them to belong to two distinct economic and political groups: Maritime and Reindeer. The first survived by hunting sea mammals and the second by herding reindeer. Leeds (1965) suggests that rather than two divisions, the Chukchi represent one basic group strategically adapted to a spatial zone including two very different habitats. The aboriginal population moved within this area responding primarily to the availability of reindeer. Since the technologies necessary to exploit both ecological zones are very different, it is possible to separate both technoeconomic adaptations and focus on one, the tending of reindeer herds, even when accepting Leeds' explanation.

Reindeer was the life source of most northern peoples, from Scandinavia to the Chukchi Peninsula on the Bering Sea. In northeastern Siberia, about 9000 Chukchi tended their domesticated herds at camps scattered over the arctic tundra. A Reindeer Chukchi camp included four to five families who herded reindeer together. The family was the socioeconomic unit, comprising a man, his wife or wives, and their children. Wives were obtained most frequently through cousin marriage since ties between persons of the same family or camp resulted in an increase of the family herds. But few men had two or more wives, for each had to be set up in a separate tent, and this required great wealth. Occasionally, several related or well-acquainted couples joined in a form of group marriage, thus profiting from sexual and economic privileges, such as the distribution of reindeer meat. However, reindeer were usually slaughtered during ceremonies. The Chukchi believed all natural objects such as forests, rivers, lakes, or animals to be animated by spirits, from which they protected the reindeer herds and themselves by wearing charms and amulets.

Technoeconomic Adaptation

The Chukchi possessed the largest reindeer herds found in northern Asia. These animals provided most survival requirements: reindeer meat was the prime source of food, the animals served to carry loads, and their skins were fashioned into clothing, tent covers, and other daily necessities. The reindeer, unlike the Tibetan yaks, were neither ridden nor milked, but like most pastoralists, the Chukchi also hunted and fished to supplement their diet.

Animal Husbandry

Animal Maintenance
   Training Herds
      deantlering reindeer: *urine vessel*/saw
      training reindeer and dogs: sled/animal-sled halter/taming club/whip
   Regulating Herd Size
      gelding reindeer (dogs): *lasso*/gelding sinew (knife)
      rounding up reindeer: snowshoes (staff)/*lasso*/*urine vessel*/*corral*/halters and traces

moving herds: pack sled/driving sled/whip/reindeer spacer/*urine vessel*/dog sled/dog whip/dog-groin protector/dog boots/raft
Protecting Herds
hobbling dogs: dog sled (stake)/rope/dog collar sticks/dog collar
hobbling reindeer: *leather hobble* (wood halter)
Food Harvest
slaughtering: *lasso/knife*
cutting antler velvet: *lasso/knife*
milking: *lasso/milk container*

The usual means to attract reindeer was with human urine, kept inside a *leather vessel* (Fig. 13) hanging from each herder's belt or sled. Reindeer used for traction were deantlered with metal-bladed *saws*. These animals were only partially domesticated and they commonly reverted to a wild state if they mingled with wild herds. A fawn was trained to pull a sled by harnessing it at the rear of a line of conveyances. The herders attached the reindeer to a *sled* in front by a *rope* bound to a *club*, and when the animal disobeyed commands the driver jerked the reins to punish it. A two-year-old pup was trained in a few months by harnessing it next to an older dog and attaching it by a *line* to a trace ahead.

A common measure taken to regulate herd size, that had the additional effect of making the bucks more tractable, was to geld the male reindeer. After catching the animal with a *lasso*, a herder tied a *sinew thread* around its testicles. Sometimes, he simply bit the spermatic ducts. Dogs were castrated with an iron *knife*.

The Chukchi transferred the reindeer herds to good pasturelands in order to feed them. During the course of a year, each camp was moved seasonally over a territory of about 150 miles. Prior to a move the herds were rounded up, and in winter the trampling of the animals' hoofs made it necessary for the herders to walk on oval-shaped *snowshoes*. During the summer moves on the tundra, a pastoralist used a short *walking stick* tipped with antler spikes. A Chukchi captured the lead animals with a *lasso* and attracted the rest of the herd with his *urine vessel*. The lasso was the most typical pastoralist subsistant and it consisted of a long, plaited, sealskin line with a noose at one end, rubbed with blubber to make it pliable (Fig. 14). The lured animals were directed into an ingenious *corral*, made by placing the sleds in a horseshoe fashion with shovels, sticks, and skins covering the gaps. When all the reindeer were inside, the entrance was closed with a rope, the animals were tied to the sleds with *halters and traces*, and the camp was ready to move. The tents and other equipment were transported on *pack sleds* drawn by a line of paired animals attached to one another by ropes. The people travelled on *driving sleds*, each pulled by a pair of reindeer. In order to prevent the reindeer from jostling each other, a herder fit a *wood block* with bone prongs on the body of one animal to prick the second if it drew close. And since reindeer are strongly drawn to urine, a *vessel* filled with this substance was attached to each *sled* to keep the animals from running wild. They were further controlled with *whips*; one variety consisted of a willow rod capped with a walrus tooth and another was a stick with a leather thong attached. Dogs served primarily as draft animals, but they were also sacrificed in ceremonies and eaten in times of famine. Because of their hardiness, they were preferred to reindeer on long journeys. On these occasions, additional dogs were borrowed from relatives, resulting at times in teams of

40   PASTORALISTS

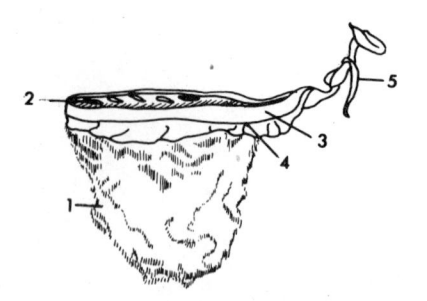

Figure 13. Reindeer Chukchi urine vessel. 1. leather bag, 2. sinew sewing stitches, 3. leather rim, 4. sinew sewing stitches, 5. leather strap. (After Bogoras 1904–1909.)

20 animals. To control their dogs, the Reindeer Chukchi used three varieties of *whips*; one was simply a stick and the others had long, leather thongs. The groins of male dogs and the bellies of suckling females were protected during storms with soft skin pieces and the feet of sled dogs were fitted with *skin boots*. During a long journey, the migrating Chukchi traversed mountain rivers with *rafts*, improvised by piling several sleds on top of each other and waterproofing them with tent covers. A lone traveller, resting overnight, tied his dogs to the *sled* or a *stake*, with *ropes* attached to *sticks* placed on their *collars* in order to prevent them from gnawing the halter. When one reindeer driver stopped at night, he either tied the animals' front feet loosely with leather *hobbles* or placed *wood halters* on the animals' necks. No other protective measures were reported.

Two men, or women, cooperated to slaughter the reindeer: one caught and held the animal with a *lasso* and the other seized it by its antlers and stabbed it through the heart with a *knife*. The aboriginal Chukchi knives were made of bone, stone, or ivory which later were replaced by iron knives. In order to keep the herd size at an optimum, reindeer seldom were slaughtered. If a herder became very hungry, he removed pieces of a male reindeer's antler velvet, presumably with a *knife*, and ate the thick outer skin. The milk produced by the does was sufficient only for fawns, therefore the reindeer were only occasionally milked, a task accomplished by striking a female down and hitting her udder with the fist to induce the release of milk. The herder sucked the udder and spit the milk into a *container*.

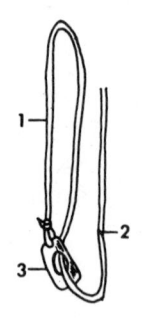

Figure 14. Reindeer Chukchi lasso. 1. plaited sealskin strap, 2. sinew sewing stitches, 3. bone eye noose. (After Bogoras 1904–1909.)

Hunting

wild-game hunting: sled/whip/*lasso*
mountain-sheep hunting: dogs/*lasso*
polar-bear hunting: driving sled/whip/*lance*
brown-bear hunting 1: *spiked-block trap/spear*

brown-bear hunting 2: log block/*spear*
winter-reindeer hunting: snowshoes/*bow and arrow*/bow wrist guard/ivory thumbguard
decoy-reindeer hunting: decoy reindeer/holding rope/tree blind/*bow and arrow*/bow wrist guard/ivory thumbguard
swimming-reindeer hunting: skin canoe/*lance* (paddle spear)
duck and geese hunting: skin canoe/*dart*
duck hunting: skin canoe/hands

---

sling
ptarmigan net
ptarmigan snare
bolas
sea-fowl snare
small-game snare
set bow

Big-game hunting provided a significant portion of the protein intake. Wild sheep, black bear, wolverine, and wolves were pursued in *sleds* and *lassoed* while mountain sheep were held at bay by the *dogs* until a herdsman could *lasso* them. On his *sled*, the herder often carried a *lance* with which to hunt polar bear. Brown bear were obtained with *traps* consisting of wood blocks with spikes covered by fallen leaves. When a bear stepped on a block, the spikes wounded its foot, which made it easier for a hunter to *spear* the animal. In winter, a herder blocked the entrance to a brown-bear's den with *logs* and *speared* it through a hole in the roof. The wild reindeer was pursued on long, thin *snowshoes* and hunted with *bows and arrows*. The sinew-backed Chukchi bow shaft was reinforced with birch bark or sinew cables glued on and a baleen piece tied to the shaft's underside; two bone pieces, attached to the shaft and separated from the bowstring by small wood supports, formed the nocks. The hunter protected his wrist and thumb with *ivory guards*. The large variety of arrows manufactured differed only in the points. A sinew wrapping or bone cap prevented the shaft's tip from splitting, and one to three feathers were either glued or tied on. Sometimes, a wild reindeer was attracted within *arrow* range by a live *reindeer decoy* which the concealed hunter controlled with a *rope*. During the summer, the hunters intercepted wild reindeer at river crossings in skin *canoes* and killed them by the hundreds, either with *lances* or *paddles* fitted with small, iron points.

Judging by the diversity of implements and facilities employed to hunt birds, these must have contributed significantly to the food supply. From their skin *canoes*, the Chukchi shot moulting ducks and geese with *darts* projected by hand. A dart had a bone point bound to the shaft with sinew, and halfway down the shaft three bone prongs were attached (Fig. 15). The men also pursued swans on lakes in their *canoes* and killed them by twisting their necks. The subsistants described next were all employed alone, including a *sling* to shoot land birds, a *snare*, and a *net*, suspended from a tree and lowered by a hunter when a ptarmigan attempted to eat the bait placed underneath. Other birds were caught with *bolas*, four or five bone or ivory balls attached to a handle by rather long strings. A

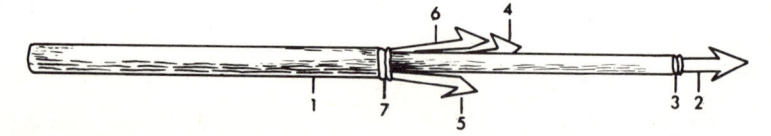

Figure 15. Reindeer Chukchi bird dart. 1. wood shaft, 2. central prong, 3. central prong-shaft sinew binder, 4–6. side prongs, 7. side prongs-shaft sinew binder. (After Bogoras 1904–1909.)

variety of *snares* were set in the water to catch fowl and of these, the most complex consisted of two baleen nooses bound to a stick and inserted in two goose quills, to keep them apart. The trapped birds were drawn to the shore by means of a long line that was attached to the stick. Marmots and squirrels were also captured in *snares*, and to hunt ermine the Chukchi employed a *set bow*. The wood bow was attached to a vertically-set rectangular frame and the blunt "arrow" was placed between the bowstring and a horizontal stick. The trigger was underneath and when an ermine touched it, the released arrow with the attached cross-piece shot downwards, strangling the animal.

Fishing

ice fishing: ice pick/*gill net*/ice scoop

fishhook
gorge
fish harpoon dart
hoop net

Despite Bogoras' comment that fish were not abundant along the coast, he described a number of fishing facilities. But only one association was reported: setting the winter *gill net* under the ice. The net was placed in the water through the chipped holes that were kept free of ice with the aid of netted *scoops*. Individual fishing must have been important since several varieties of *fishhooks* were reported. The most complex was used in salt water without a rod, and consisted of several ivory pieces with hooks, each connected by a thong to a sinker. The Chukchi manufactured a burbot-catching *gorge* by tying a line to a pointed, wood shank and placing a bait on it. A *harpoon dart* with a detachable hook was used to fish grayling and trout, and during the summer they suspended *hoop nets* by ropes from river posts and held them inside the water with stone sinkers, to fish.

Storants

The Reindeer Chukchi possessed a number of specialized storants. The receptacles were predominantly flexible, and included large reindeer-skin bags to hold frozen blood and smaller bags for blubber. A reindeer bladder was designed to hold the rarely obtained milk, and water was continuously available by filling with ice a wood receptacle which the herders hung inside the tent, collecting the melted water in a dish placed underneath. When the members of a camp were ready to move to their summer pastures, they slaughtered about a dozen reindeer to have food for the trail. The meat was temporarily placed in a pit dug in the middle of the tent floor and covered with sod until their departure. Sometimes, after having butchered the fattest wild reindeer bucks, the Chukchi hung the meat on the branches of trees. In order to keep meat for long periods, they excavated a pit in the frozen soil beneath a tent and covered it with skins and grass. Very large reindeer-skin bags were utilized to store meat, intestines, blood, and blood-based edibles. The only artifactual, structural storant was the dome-shaped tent, where all foods were stored for long periods of time in the space between its outer and inner frames.

Analysis

The Reindeer Chukchi possessed 24 subsistants, of which 50 percent were used to hunt and only 25 percent to tend the herds. The remainder were used to fish and gather wild foods. By contrast with the Tibetans, who used all facilities but one to tend the animals, the 17 Chukchi facilities served almost equally to hunt, fish, and take care of the herds. Apparently, herding was relatively more important for the high plateau nomads than the arctic pastoralists.

The total number of Chukchi subsistant components (153) was much greater than that of the Tibetans (63). Suggestively, the material culture complexity is more accurately measured by components than individual types. The Tibetans had 16 and the Chukchi 24. How can the complexity of the Chukchi subsistants be explained? Although the most complex subsistant was the bow and arrow, an implement with 25 parts, the total number of components making up the facilities (94) was larger than that which comprised the implements (59). Thus, we must rule out the possibility that the total number of subsistant components was influenced by the most complex form. On the other hand, the Chukchi possessed a great number of facilities, which might be the reason for the greater facility component number compared to that found for the implements. Seven of the facilities were employed to hunt, five to tend domestic animals, and five to fish, which agrees with the information on the mixed character of the Reindeer Chukchi economy. This fact may also explain the greater complexity of the Chukchi nomads' subsistants compared to those of the Tibetan herders. Apparently, the greater the number of alternative resources the more complex the technology. Furthermore, the fact that the most complex subsistant was employed to hunt reinforces the suggestion made in the Tibetan analysis that greater manufacturing expenditures are required to forage than to herd, due to the nature of both occupations.

The predominantly cold climate allowed the Chukchi to store food and their mobility made it highly desirable, since during a move it was sometimes difficult to forage for food. Of the nine Chukchi storants, three were specialized reindeer-meat containers, supporting the postulate that a greater diversity of storage forms was associated with the main dietary item of a culture. The Reindeer Chukchi had even more specialized storants than the Tibetans, and the range of storant components was greater among the Chukchi than the high plateau nomads. The short-term storants were manufactured with 1 to 3 components, while the long-term containers had a minimum of 3 and a maximum of 28 parts.

The Reindeer Chukchi had far more associations than the Tibetans. 47 percent of the 21 technotasks concerned hunting, and 47 percent focused on animal husbandry while 5 percent represented the fishing tasks. Although the Reindeer Chukchi were considered to have depended heavily on their domesticated herds, the strategic variability to obtain wild game was identical to that observed with herding. Furthermore, the greater resource alternatives of the Chukchi, in contrast with those of the Tibetans, resulted in a greater variety of technoeconomic activities, as well as the greater structural complexity of their subsistants. Judging by the number of associations used in both tribes to harvest the domestic foods, few alternatives were possible. Both tribes represent cases of pastoralists whose dependence on the domesticated herds differed greatly. Yet, the most complex technotask in both tribes was the movement of the herds, which was accomplished by the Reindeer Chukchi with ten subsistants and aids in association in comparison with the six used by the Tibetans. Once again, it appears that societies subsisting at the same economic level differed greatly in all aspects of their material culture, the strategic variability to exploit their resources, and the degree of dependence on each.

TABLE 6. PASTORAL TIBETAN AND REINDEER CHUKCHI SUBSISTANTS

	Tibet	Chukchi
Artifact		
implement		
instrument		
simple	sickle(2) hoe(3) knife(3)	digging pick(4)
weapon		
simple	slaughtering rope(1) spear(8)	slaughtering knife(3) paddle spear (3) (1 var.) lance(5) bird dart(7)
complex	sling(6) bow and arrow(9)	sling(12) bow and arrow(25)
facility		
tended		
simple	milking hook and pail(8)	milk container(2) lasso(3) urine vessel(5) fishhook(5) (3 var.) ptarmigan net(7) sea-fowl snare(8) (4 var.) seine(12) (1 var.)
complex	game trap(7)	gorge(3) harpoon dart(3) bolas(4)
untended		
simple	hobble(1) cattle pen(1) sheepfold(2) stall(2) fetters(3)	halter(2) (1 var.) spiked block trap(3) small-game snare(4) ptarmigan snare(5) reindeer corral(6) hoop net(9) (1 var.)
complex	calf tether(3) cow tether(4)	set bow(13)

TABLE 7. PASTORAL TIBETAN AND REINDEER CHUKCHI STORANTS

	Tibet	*Chukchi*
Naturefact		
structure		
short-term		tree(1)
Artifact		
receptacle		
short-term	goatskin(1)	milk container(2)
	yak-hair cloth(1)	blood bag(3)
	butter box(2)	gravel pit(3)
	sour-milk tub(3)	
long-term	yak (sheep) stomach(2)	food bag(3)
	leather bag(5)	blubber bag(3)
		frozen pit(4)
		water container(6)
structure		
long-term	tent(17)	tent(28)

CASE STUDY INTERACTIONS

1. Are there any significant differences between the technotasks and subsistants of pastoralists who were dependent on different animal species? What are they? For example, you may compare the Tibetan yak and sheep herders with the Reindeer Chukchi and the Navajo sheep, goat, cattle, and horse pastoralists.

2. Using the information in this chapter, alter the pastoralist associations. A useful source is *The Barabaig: East African Cattle Herders* (Klima, 1970). For example, introduce an alternative classification of the nomads' activities, or rearrange the ordering of the technotasks according to any criteria you consider significant. Try to convey the maximum information possible, but minimize unnecessary details.

4
Farmers[1]

AO NAGA

Rice was the staple of the 30,000 Ao Naga headhunters occupying northeastern Assam. Swift mountain streams crossed the deep, cultivated valleys, and the virgin soils were covered by evergreen forests and dense jungle vegetation. Wild elephants, pigs, deer, and monkeys ranged the hillsides as well as the numerous domesticated and wild varieties of hill cattle or mithan.

The social, political, and religious unit of the Ao was the village, a house cluster built on a hilltop, surrounded by a protective fence and light jungle vegetation. The villages were permanent, for the Ao preferred to cultivate fields located three to four miles away rather than to move. Long ago, feuds between Ao villages resulted in wars, and to pay off debts and war indemnities, the headhunting Aos took slaves. The strictly exogamous marriages represented one way by which the threat of war was reduced, since marriage partners had to be found outside one of the three Ao clans. Marriages were not ceremonially consummated, but the event was marked by an exchange of gifts between the two families. This set the pattern for all the future relationships between in-laws and lessened the possibility of wars breaking out between their separate clans and neighboring villages. In almost all Ao ceremonies, mithan or hill cattle were sacrificed. A harvest festival was celebrated at the beginning rather than at the end of the harvest. Presumably this was to provide the cultivators with added proteins, since during the ceremony cattle and pigs were slaughtered. Among the chief means to obtain social status was the organization by individuals of feasts of merit, a series of ceremonies which ended with the mithan sacrifices. To symbolize the economic integration of a boy into the community, his father gave a small feast. Girls were ritually introduced through a series of tatooing ceremonies which began when they were ten years old and ended five years later. Several funeral feasts were also organized while a dead person's body was being burned. The Ao believed in a number of gods, but most characteristically they worshipped natural boulders in which most spirits were presumed to reside. Once a year, each village held a ceremony in the honor of these boulders, beginning with a pig sacrifice and leading to the distribution of pork.

---

[1] Most of the Ao Naga data was obtained from Mills (1926) and Smith (1925). Pospisil's (1963a) excellent monograph was the main source consulted for the material culture and subsistence information on the Kapauku Papuans.

Technoeconomic Adaptation

The Ao had limited barter with the Hindu peasants of the Assamese plains, from whom they obtained salt and iron in exchange for spices, cotton, and bamboo mats. Rice was the Ao staple, cultivated without the aid of animal traction despite the fact that domesticated animals were raised. Although Murdock (1967) reports that only 6 to 15 percent of the subsistence was based on foraging, numerous hunting and fishing strategies were recorded.

Plant Cultivation

rice farming: dao/hoe/fence/fire/logs/planting stick/weeding hoe/aqueduct/*sickle* /*reaping basket*/big collecting basket

chilli farming: dao/hoe/fence/fire/planting stick/weeding hoe/baked-earth manure/*sickle* (dao)

The shifting cultivation method used by the Aos is called "jhum" and, reportedly, its results were so excellent that famines rarely occurred. A village usually exploited a single block of land, divided into family plots that were cultivated for two consecutive years and then left fallow for ten years. The hillside jungles were cut down with *daos*, commonly described as "chopping knives," that served multiple purposes. A dao was employed as a tool to carve house posts and cut cane, an aid in agricultural pursuits, a weapon of offense in war, and a subsistant to sacrifice mithans and kill boars, monkeys, and bears. The dao had a broad, socketed, iron blade, sharpened only on one curved edge and fitted into a bamboo or wood handle to which it was attached with a rattan binder (Fig. 16). The dao was carried inside a wood holder hanging from the belt. A previously-cleared field was weeded with a *hoe*, the main cultivating instrument. Balfour (1917) identified different varieties of Naga hoes as developments on a primitive type, still utilized at the time of contact. The original form consisted of one piece of bamboo with crossed ends that were bound together (Fig. 17).

The men sowed the seeds in the fields that had been cleared in previous years and *fenced* them in to protect them from roaming pigs. After the rainy season, when the plant cover had dried sufficiently, the men set the jungle on *fire*, and

Figure 16. Ao Naga dao. 1. *iron blade*, 2. *bamboo handle*, 3. *blade-handle rattan binder*. (From The Ao Nagas by J. P. Mills. Copyright 1926 by The Macmillan Company.)

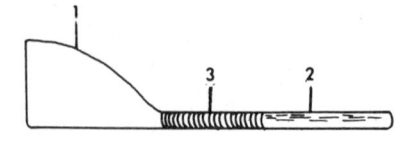

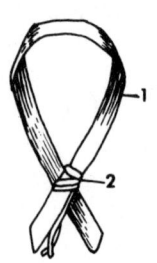

Figure 17. Ao Naga hoe (*aid*). 1. bamboo blade, 2. cane binder. (After Balfour 1917.)

with their *hoes* mixed the ashes into the soil to fertilize it. Each man constructed a field house next to his plot and built a special structure in front of his dwelling to hold the ceremonial offerings, usually egg- and fowl-filled baskets. Next, he laid lines of *logs* to check the erosion, after which the women, aided with their *planting sticks*, sowed the rice seeds. Quite commonly, an Ao woman weeded her family's garden five times a year with a small, semicircular *hoe*.

If a field was far from a stream or spring, the Aos built a bamboo *aqueduct* that brought water from long distances and emptied into a wood *trough*. When the rice ears began to appear, the men built the threshing floors behind their field houses and the women and elder men reaped the grain with small, curved, serrated *sickles*. With one movement of the arm, they threw the grain inside the conical *baskets* that hung from their backs. The younger men walked from harvester to harvester with larger *baskets* in which they collected the rice and carried it to the threshing floors. Here, they trampled on the grain with their feet, winnowed it with fans, and after measuring the harvest in special baskets, they stored it in granaries. After a few weeks, the cycle recommenced, with the men cutting down the virgin jungle to prepare the new plots.

Taro, a root crop, was grown in patches among the rice, mainly to feed the pigs. The planting, harvesting, and drying of this tuber was the responsibility of women. Other plants, grown in small, fenced-in gardens, included maize, ginger, gourds, cucumbers, and considerable quantities of sweet potatoes. Only two crops, chillies and lentils, required additional care. The soil in which chillies were planted was fertilized with *baked earth* gathered from under the burnt jungle logs, and the lentil stems were cut with *daos* to ensure that the whole plant would ripen at the same time. Betel was mostly grown for the lowland trade.

Animal Husbandry

Animal Maintenance
   Regulating Herd Size
      feeding pigs: *pigsty*/food trough
      gelding pigs: dao/soot/needle and thread
      branding pigs (dogs): knife
   Protecting Herds
      pig and cattle confinement: *compound*
      hen confinement: house/*nesting basket*
Food Harvest
      pig and cattle slaughter: *halter*/house/*dao*
      hen slaughter: *dao*

Pigs, cattle, and mithan were the main domestic animals, slaughtered for their meat but not used as sources of work or milk. Each village had numerous pigs to do most of the scavenging. Each pig owner lodged his animals in the outer room of the house, which thus functioned temporarily as a *pigsty*. Here he kept a feeding *trough* filled with taro and rice, and every morning the household head opened a small door to let the pigs out. When the boars were about two years old they were castrated, presumably with a *dao*, and the wound was cauterized with *soot* and sewn with a bamboo *needle and thread*. At that time, the ears of a pig were cut with a *knife* to identify their owner. The Aos kept dogs almost exclusively to eat, especially male puppies. Their ears and tails were docked with *knives* and the cut portions hung on the house's walls as decoration.

In order to avoid damage to the crops, few sacrificial mithan were kept around a village, but common cattle were bred in large numbers for their meat. Although cattle were allowed to roam at will during the day, at night they were confined in *compounds*, presumably built with stakes near each house. Inside his *house* an Ao placed *bamboo nests* on the walls to protect the hens from rats. The night before the pigs and domesticated cattle were to be slaughtered they were bound by fiber *halters* to the *house*, and the following day they were killed with *daos*. Numerous goats were raised for their meat and hair. Sheep were less numerous, since they could not flourish in the restrictive grazing grounds available.

Hunting

deer hunting 1: *pitfall/spear*
deer hunting 2: *snare/spear*
deer hunting 3: dogs/*spear*
bear hunting: *spear/dao*
elephant hunting 1: *pitfall/spear*
elephant hunting 2: *spear trap/spear*
monkey hunting 1: *tunnel trap/spear*
monkey hunting 2: *monkey fall trap/dao*
monkey hunting 3: *dao/spear*
individual boar hunting: footprint measure/bridge/*spear/dao*
communal boar hunting: dao (fire)/*corral*/platform/*spear/dao*

blowgun
bow and arrow
bird lime stick
bird snares in fence
crossbow

Large game was obtained using a variety of strategies and techniques, several of which involved hunting deer. At a known deer crossing an Ao dug a *pitfall* and camouflaged it with saplings and leaves. At the bottom he placed bamboo spikes which impaled the trapped animal, later killed with a *spear*. The spear was the hunting weapon used with the greatest frequency, and the most complex variety had a diamond-shaped iron point, with a socket which fitted into a wood shaft and was attached to it by a vine binder. A double-edged blade, fastened to the shaft's butt, served as a walking aid and to hold the spear upright on the ground in order to avoid blunting the point. An Ao also snared deer using a bent branch connected by a rope to a trigger mechanism on the ground. After the animal disturbed the trigger, its leg became entangled in the *snare*. Sometimes, deer were pursued with *dogs*, although these animals were preferred as food rather than hunting companions. On rare occasions the men hunted bear. These animals more often found the hunters than the other way around, and when they charged, they were wounded with *spears* and killed with *daos*. Elephants were taken by digging a series of small holes along their trails, and at the bottom the hunter placed flat stones to support upright iron spikes. The *pits* were covered with earth and an unsuspecting elephant injured by the spikes was easily tracked and *speared*. Another method used to hunt elephants consisted of tying a spear by a rope to the ground. A triggering mechanism released the *spear trap* whenever an animal tripped on it.

Monkeys were also hunted in various ways. An ingenious *tunnel trap*, in which up to 50 animals could be taken in one day, consisted of a gully roofed along its length, presumably with bamboo, and closed at one end. The cornered, stump-tailed macaques were *speared*. In his fields, an Ao placed a *bamboo box*, with a cucumber bait attached to a stone-covered shelf that fell on the trespassing macaques. The men climbed high trees to capture monkeys and cut down the branches with their *daos*.

Boars were hunted by individuals as a sport rather than a basic subsistence activity. The hunter who discovered an animal's footprints measured them with *bamboo sticks*, thus ensuring future ownership of the beast. Sometimes a particular boar was intermittently tracked for two or three years! In their boar-tracking travels, the Aos occasionally encountered a valley stream that they crossed with a *bridge* consisting of a bamboo ladder, attached on one bank to the overhanging branches of a tree, joined to a tree trunk on the other bank to facilitate the crossing. When the hunter finally discovered "his" boar, he *speared* it and killed it with his *dao*. Despite the reports that wild pigs were mainly slaughtered to eliminate their potential danger to the rice crops, they were also communally hunted for food. When a group of hunters found a herd, they surrounded it and cleared a patch of jungle around it with their *daos*, or built a *fire* instead. This circle was gradually closed, forcing the pigs to enter an adjacent *corral* built with brushwood and stakes. On top of the fence they constructed small *platforms* from which the older men and women guided the herds. The younger hunters injured the pigs with their *spears* and killed them with their *daos*. In one successful hunt, members of a village slaughtered 80 pigs in one day, causing great excitement. Sometimes, something went wrong and the whole herd escaped.

Besides these hunting practices, which required the employment of at least two material forms, the Aos utilized a variety of subsistants individually. For instance, children used a *blowgun* to kill birds; this weapon consisted of a hollow, bamboo tube with two seeds fitted at each end. A plunger was inserted in one extremity, forcing one seed through the tube, compressing the air, and expelling the second seed.

More commonly, birds were reportedly shot with *bows and arrows*, although one authority (Fraser 1922) comments that the weapon was not indigenous to the Naga. A more ordinary way to capture birds was with a long, *bamboo stick* covered with boiled rubber sap and tied lightly to a tree's branch. In its struggle to free its glued feet, a bird fell to the ground. Birds were also trapped in *snares* placed on gaps along *fences*, or fine *nooses* arranged on the ground around flowers. Small game and monkeys were reportedly hunted with the *crossbow*, considered by Hutton (1921) to be an eastern introduction that was beginning to replace the bow and arrow, but presumed by Mills (1926) and Smith (1925) to be an obsolete Naga weapon. Since not one of the Ao ethnographers gave structural details of the crossbow I have borrowed Hutton's description for the Sema Naga. On one end of a grooved wood stock rested a bamboo feathered arrow, while on the other a bone lock served to release the string that rested on the arrow's butt. The trigger turned on a pin that crossed the lock from side to side and was released by pressure of the forefinger (Fig. 18).

Fishing

fishing 1: *dam*/dao holder/bamboo dish/hands
fishing 2: *dam and platform*/mud/*poisonous vine*/beating sticks/splashing sticks/ *dipnet* (dao, hands)
fishing 3: *walnut leaf poison*/bank hollow/ beating sticks/mud/poison basket/ *dipnet* (dao, hands)
fishing 4: *two weirs*/beating sticks/*bark poison*/dao holder/*dipnet* (hands)

fishhook

About once a year, the members of a village went to a mountain stream to fish, believing that fishing would bring rain. It is interesting that, among the Aos, two subsistence activities, fishing and farming, were conceptually linked in their supernatural system. A very commonly practiced fishing method consisted of *damming* a tributary river. With their *dao holders* the men splashed the water upstream and dried the channel with *bamboo dishes*, picking up the trapped fish with their *hands*. Sometimes they *dammed* a stream with a log topped by a *platform* and covered with a series of layers of *mud* and previously-pounded *poisonous vines*. The mud obscured the waters, and was believed to increase the poison's effectiveness. The men introduced the deadly mixture into the water with *sticks* and gathered the stupefied fish with *dipnets*, *daos*, or *hands*. *Walnut leaves* were a second source of poison. In *small hollows* scooped out on river banks, the Aos inserted the plant and beat it with *sticks* to obtain the poisonous pulp that they placed, together with the *mud*, in wide-meshed *baskets*. The men formed a line across a shallow river and swung the baskets back and forth to scatter their contents; the stunned fish were gathered as before. Sometimes they built on one of two tributary streams two parallel *weirs* with bamboo, wood, and mud to divert most of the water into the second channel. Then they introduced a *tree-bark poison* in the isolated fork, whose waters were extracted with *dao holders*, and collected the stunned fish with *dipnets*. The use of *fishhooks* was quite uncommon among the Ao Nagas, yet ethnographers found in their possession a simple hook baited with a live grasshopper or worm attached to a twisted, fibre line.

Storants

The storing technology of cereal agriculturalists was expected to be quite developed, mainly because grain harvests are seasonal. The Ao data supports the suggestion, for these people employed eight different storants. Water was temporarily placed in bamboo sections on the walls of a house and rice beer was stored in bottle gourds. The wells were fenced and roofed over to prevent the entrance of pigs and the falling of leaves. Every two to three years these natural springs were

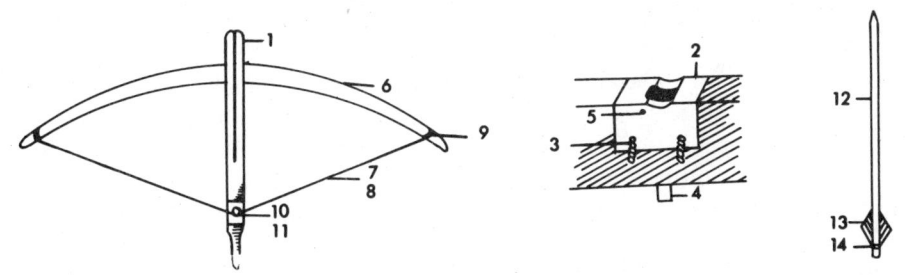

Figure 18. Ao Naga crossbow. 1. wood stock, 2. bone lock, 3. stock-lock cane binder, 4. trigger, 5. trigger-pin hole, 6. wood shaft, 7. fiber bowstring, 8. bowstring oil, 9. shaft-bowstring cane binder, 10. bowstring-lock cane binder, 11. arrow-positioning pin, 12. bamboo arrow shaft, 13. bamboo-spathe feathering, 14. feathering-shaft cane binder. (From The Sema Nagas by J. H. Hutton. Copyright 1921 by The Macmillan Company.)

redug. Although these people were primarily farmers, they obtained abundant proteins from domesticated and wild animal species. They kept meat temporarily in bamboo baskets inside the house, in the space between the ceiling and the roof. Dried meat and fish were placed on skewers and stored for long periods. Some of the meat was smoked and kept on bamboo trays hanging from the ceiling on top of the fire. Rice, the staple, was stored in baskets, but specialized structures were also used. The granaries were small, raised houses built on the outskirts of each village. Along the path from the fields to the villages temporary sheds were constructed. Often one corner of the main room of a house was partitioned off to serve as a general storeroom, and sometimes food was stored in the outer room of a house.

Analysis

Among the 25 Ao subsistants, a relatively great number were complex manufactures used in hunting. Counting the components in each taxonomic class, the untended, complex hunting facilities had more parts (36) than any other group. Both simple and complex subsistants were made to take the same animal species, indicating a specialization in hunting methods. Furthermore, the most complex subsistant, with 14 components, was the hunting crossbow. Considering that the Ao depended mainly on farming, the diversity of hunting subsistants was surprising. However, all of these findings suggest that *incipient horticulturalists, who also depended on wild animal foods, developed their animal-taking equipment more than aboriginal hunters who did not also farm.* The lightening of the food quest that followed the cultivation of plants presumably allowed further experimentation with the hunting subsistants available. A proliferation of instruments to harvest the crops might be expected among settled farmers. But the facts are otherwise. I did not find any reference to a digging stick with which to gather vegetable foods.

Their storing technology was, on the other hand, quite varied. Five specialized storants were used: the rice granaries and sheds, the meat trays, rice-beer bottle gourds, water containers, and two diversified storants in which various foods were kept—the baskets and the house. As expected, the storing technology of these cereal cultivators was quite specialized. A brief consideration of the supernatural, or ceremonial component of survival may add to our understanding of the relationship between the material culture and other social behaviors. In a sense, food-quest uncertainties were greater among plant cultivators than among foragers. The hunter's and gatherer's success largely depended on his knowledge of the territory and habits of his prey, and the availability of edible species. By depending mainly on his own skills, the only major remaining uncertainty was game abundance. Farmers, on the other hand, had a greater resource control in the sense that they determined what was to be planted, when, and how. But the environmental insecurities were greater than those faced by the hunters. The needed amounts of rain could differ from the annual or seasonal precipitation available, the presence of strong winds or frozen soils could be harmful to the crops, and so on, dependent on the area or cultigen under consideration. By contrast with the environmental prerequisites, the strategies that farmers could apply were minimal. The general uncertainty caused by these factors must have given rise to the propitiatory ceremonies characteristic of horticultural societies, of which a most common example are those staged to bring rain.

These comments should not be read as a denial of the greater potential of farming societies to feed larger and larger populations, in comparison with foraging groups. The stress here is not on the long-range effects of each major strategy, but the synchronic adaptations observed in each. That is, the phenomena are studied as representing one particular point in time, without regard to their past or future implications. The main presumption in this study is the fact that all cultural phenomena have material correlates; therefore one would expect a profusion of ceremonial objects to be manufactured where involvement with the supernatural was very marked. Despite the absence of a universal classification, the material productions of a tribe may be roughly grouped into logical categories. Tools are separated from containers, ornaments, musical instruments, ceremonial paraphernalia, and so on. And whereas the Aos procured food with 25 subsistants and kept it in 8 storants, 42 ceremonial objects were reported, almost doubling the subsistant inventory and confirming the ethnographic reports of their great ceremonial involvement.

A total of 21 technotasks were recorded, of which 52 percent involved hunting, 19 percent focused on animal husbandry and fishing, and only 9 percent represented farming activities. The Ao employed fewer strategies to farm than to fish or tend the herds; most activities focused on hunting. Yet the most complex technoeconomic task, in terms of numbers of subsistants and aids, was rice farming, with 11 forms used in association. Thus the Ao's greatest technological involvement was with their focal survival activity. Subsistants were used to produce food directly, whereas aids complemented their use in survival activities. Could it be that the relative use of these two material culture clusters varied, dependent on the activity in which they were employed? To ascertain the truth of this suggestion, I calculated the relative percentages of subsistants and aids in each technotask, considering the appearance of a form only once. The results are shown in the following table:

	Subsistants (in percentages)	*Aids* (in percentages)
farming	27.27	72.72
hunting	64.28	35.71
fishing	33.33	66.66
animal husbandry	40.00	60.00

While aids appear to be increasingly important in farming activities, the subsistants decrease in significance, but they are most often used to hunt, with a concomitant decrease in hunting aids. The results are not as significant among fishing and animal husbandry activities, yet in the four cases there is an inverse use of subsistants and aids. One reason may be the different relationships that are involved between men and the environment in each subsistence activity. Where humans exert a greater control over the resources, aids predominate. Subsistants proliferate in the context of lesser external dominance in which there is a necessary dependence on objects explicitly functioning to procure food, as the conditions of its availability cannot be purposefully altered.

KAPAUKU PAPUANS

The tropical forest of Western New Guinea supported 45,000 Kapauku Papuans who depended mainly on the cultivation of root crops for food. High mountains and deep valleys predominated in the region. A typical village had 15 houses inhabited by 120 people, and each household included from 5 to 40 individuals who were not necessarily related. It was common for a man to have several wives and the polygynous family represented the productive unit. A man searched for a wife outside his sib, and the wars that usually originated from disputes over a woman were more common between groups of Kapauku who intermarried than between groups who did not. Thus, the culture provided a mechanism to regulate aggression since where strong ties existed, such as those established between intermarrying families, the disruptive nature of wars could be sustained. In contrast, fighting was less common between groups not related by marriage, since these wars may have caused too many deaths, resulting in unfavorable population decreases.

The Kapauku, unlike most aboriginal societies, developed a monetary system comparable to that known in Western civilization. It was based on cowrie shells and cowrie-shell necklaces. With his money, a Kapauku could obtain anything and everything, from meat to land, women, prestige, and power. The secular orientation of the culture was mirrored in their ceremonial life. No fertility rites, group initiations, or preoccupation with the dead was evident. Instead, the most elaborate ceremonial occasions focused on the sale of pigs. The main event was the pig feast, which required the construction of a dance house and of guest dwellings for the hundreds of visitors who came from distant Papuan villages. In the strictest sense, this feast concerned the distribution of pork, since hundreds of slaughtered pigs were sold, lent, and exchanged. The pig feasts also functioned to institutionalize trade. Members of different tribes exchanged a variety of raw materials for manufactured items. Kapauku culture may best be characterized by the possession of a money capitalism and extensive trade networks, but the economic foundations were based on the sweet-potato gardens and the domesticated pigs.

Technoeconomic Adaptation

Plant Cultivation

extensive-shifting cultivation: canoe/stone machete/hands/stone ax/fire/fence/fire breaks/fire/planting stick/weeding stick/hut/pointed bamboo sticks/boar-spring pole snares/boar pitfall/rat snare/*harvesting stick/reaping bag*
intensive-shifting cultivation: stone machete/hands/drainage ditch/fence/fire breaks/fire/planting stick/stone knife/sugar-cane support poles/bottle gourd structure/weeding stick/hut/rat snare/sugar-cane *harvesting knife* (sweet-potato harvesting stick/reaping bag)
intensive-complex cultivation: bridge/fertilizer/drainage ditch/fence/fire break/fire/hands/weeding stick/hut/rat snare/*earth knife*
tree cultivation: fire break/planting stick/weeding stick/*stone knife*

Because of soil and terrain differences, sweet potatoes were cultivated with different methods, one practiced on the mountain slopes and two in the valleys. On the mountains, where the vegetation cover was dense, they cultivated with extensive-shifting methods. Some of the mountain plots were located across a river and to reach them the Kapauku used their *canoes*. With a polished hand-held stone, or *machete*, a man cut the underbrush and extracted the plant remains with his *hands*. First he felled smaller trees with a *stone ax* consisting of an oval blade bound with rattan to a hollow wood handle, and then he set the roots of the larger trees on *fire* for several days. They built *fences* around cleared plots and prepared *fire breaks* before *firing* the underbrush (Fig. 19). Afterwards the women dug holes in the ground with their long, pointed *sticks* to plant the sweet-potato vines (Fig. 20). At least three times during the growing period the women weeded the gardens with short, *paddle-shaped instruments*. For the crops to be harvested, it was necessary to protect the plots from marauding animals. One protective device was a small *hut* built by a cultivator near a distant garden. He did not necessarily sleep there, because the structure alone acted as a deterrent for the thieves and pigs. Pointed *bamboo sticks* were hidden under leaf covers behind lowered fences to discourage the intrusion of pigs or men. The farmers also set wild boar and rat *spring-pole snares* and *pitfalls* for boars. The sweet-potato tubers rotted within three days and had to be harvested daily. A woman dug out the tubers with a *harvesting stick* and dropped them inside a *reaping bag* that hung on her back, suspended from her forehead. The mountain swidden cycle ended when the gardens were left to fallow from 7 to 12 years.

On the valley floor, the Kapauku practiced two types of intensive cultivation, shifting and complex. Both shared the features of a larger variety of plants grown than in the mountains, the construction of drainage ditches, and the rotation of

Figure 19. Kapauku slash-and-burn agriculture. A man runs across a field after the vegetation has been burned off. (Reprinted with permission of the Yale University Publications in Anthropology, and the author Leopold Pospisil.)

the crops. The main differences between both valley methods consisted in the application of fertilizer and, with the intensive-complex method, the planting of sweet potatoes without a stick. The intensive-shifting cultivation required the clearing of the valley undergrowth that was not as dense as on the mountains. Among the most important plants grown were sweet potatoes, sugar cane, taro, reed, spinach greens, bottle gourds, squash, yams, and cucumbers. With spadelike tools the men dug *drainage ditches*, forming rectangular plots around which they later erected *fences*. After preparing the *fire breaks*, they burned the underbrush. *Sticks* were used to *plant the* sweet-potato shoots, and to cut the taro leaves and plant the sugar-cane sections a *stone knife* was required. In addition, the sugar cane was tied to *poles* and *wood structures* were built to support the bottle-gourd vines. In the valleys the weeds grew faster than on the mountain slopes and each crop required from three to four weedings. Even though these gardens were close to the houses, protective *huts* were built and the *rat snares* were the only facilities set, since people and domesticated pigs could have been injured by the larger traps. The Kapauku harvested sweet potatoes with *sticks* and used *knives* to cut the ripe sugar cane; some cultigen or other was always ready for harvest and all garden crops were rotated before fallowing.

The third and most sophisticated cultivation method, called intensive-complex, was practiced in the valley plots where only two cultigens were grown: the sweet potato and a plant called "idaja." This manner of cultivating was most commonly applied to old swiddens where it was unnecessary to fell trees. To reach some of the gardens located on the far side of shallow streams, the Kapauku built *log bridges*. They prepared rectangular beds and covered them with rotten vegetable matter, dirt, or fresh plants to *fertilize* the soil. Around the beds they dug deep

58   FARMERS

Figure 20. Kapauku Papuan woman planting sweet-potato shoots with the help of a planting stick. (Reprinted with permission of the Yale University Publications in Anthropology, and the author Leopold Pospisil.)

drainage ditches and built a *fence* before the underbrush was fired. They planted the sweet-potato vines with their *hands* and used *sticks to weed* out the unwanted vegetation. Due to the proximity of these plots to the houses the only protective devices were *huts* and *rat snares*. Instead of the harvesting stick, a leaf-shaped hardwood implement called an *earth knife* was used to harvest the valley crops. The plots were left to fallow from one to two months and after an adequate number of rotations of the sweet-potato and "idaja" plants a fallowing period of up to eight years was common.

FARMERS

In the lowland gardens and near their houses, the Kapauku planted fruit trees, of which only the banana had some economic significance. The men cut the suckers of older trees with unmodified *stones* and planted the shoots, which yielded fruits in one and a half years. The banana trees remained productive for two decades.

Animal Husbandry

Animal Maintenance
   Regulating Herd Size
      feeding piglets: net bag/pointed stick
      feeding pigs: *pigsty*
      gelding: bamboo knife
      branding pigs: bamboo knife
Food Harvest
      pig slaughter: *bamboo knife* (arrow, club)

Besides providing proteins, pigs represented the capital through which a Kapauku could achieve wealth and political power. Despite the importance of pig breeding, very few materials were used to tend these animals. A woman usually carried a six-week-old piglet inside a *net bag* during the day and fed it prechewed food. At night she kept it in her quarters. When the pig grew older, its female owner took it to old garden plots and, using a *pointed stick*, taught it to dig for roots and grubs. When the pig was around five months old it was allowed to sleep under the elevated floor of the house, which functioned as a *pigsty*. Every morning and evening a household member fed the animals. The symbiotic relationship between pigs and men had the added advantage that the animals regularly cleaned the harvested plots which, in turn, also helped to minimize their threat to the freshly-planted gardens. *Bamboo knives* served to geld male pigs and also to brand them, by cutting off a portion of their ears or tails. Also, with these weapons the domestic pigs were eventually slaughtered.

Fishing

swamp-tadpole fishing: feet/*dipnet*/net bag (bamboo section)
open-water tadpole fishing 1: canoe/*dipnet*/net bag (bamboo section)
open-water tadpole fishing 2: two canoes/anchor/*three tadpole dipnets*/three forked sticks/stirring pole/net bag
open-water tadpole fishing 3: *dipnet*/*dam*/two canoes/stirring pole/net bag
open-water crayfish fishing 1: canoe/*forked sticks* (net)/net bag
open-water crayfish fishing 2: canoe/*dipnet*/stirring pole/net bag
baited-crayfish fishing 1: *baited dipnet*/anchor pole/net bag
baited-crayfish fishing 2: *baited stick*/canoe/*scoop*/net bag
men's-crayfish fishing: hands/net bag
night-crayfish fishing: torch/*leister*/net bag

The lakes and rivers of the region were almost devoid of fish, but their absence was compensated by the abundance of crayfish and dragonfly larvae. Fishing for these species was economically more significant than hunting and gathering because the water catches provided a reliable and continuous protein source. In swampy, shallow waters, a group of women and children stamped on the reeds and collected the emergent tadpoles with small *dipnets* that differed from the openwater nets by having a shorter handle tied to the oval frame; in both varieties the netting was made from the inner bark of several trees. The tadpole catches were immediately placed inside a *net bag* that hung on a woman's back, or in a *bamboo container* that she held in her hands. Both represent aids because they were indispensable in harvesting the small species. A fisherwoman stood on her *canoe* and dragged the *dipnet* on the bottom of a lake to collect tadpoles. Sometimes two women fished together. One stood on an anchored *canoe* with three *tadpole nets* spread against its sides and held in place by three *forked sticks*. The second woman, standing on another *canoe*, drove the tadpoles towards the waiting nets with a *pole*. Occasionally tadpoles were caught in *nets* placed at the opening of a reed or stone *dam* built across a stream. While one woman waited in her *canoe* by the net, her partner paddled slowly downstream, driving the tadpoles into the nets with her long *pole*.

In open waters, a woman pulled up bundles of weeds with a *forked stick* to collect the hiding crayfish. Sometimes two women fished from one *canoe*; one stood at one end holding the *dipnet* on the river or lake bottom, and the second drove the crayfish into the net with a *pole* by walking from the far corner of the boat towards the other woman. A sweet-potato or lizard bait was sometimes attached to a *dipnet*, which was driven into the river after tying it to the forked end of a stick that was bound to a *pole* placed slantwise on a river bank (Fig. 21). Another fishing technique consisted of tying a dead frog or lizard to the forked end of a *stick* that was inserted in the water either from a *canoe* or a river bank; the lured crayfish were collected with a small *scoop net* bound to a round frame.

Fishing was a sport for the men, who occasionally caught the crayfish that had become entangled in the river vegetation with their *hands*. Sometimes a group of men, carrying dried reed *torches*, speared the crayfish at night with five pronged, hardwood *leisters*.

Hunting

python hunting: *stones/club*
boar hunting: hands/*club*
grass-fire hunting: fire/*club* (bow and arrow)/net bag
rat hunting: island/feet/*bow and arrow*
fruit-bat hunting: banana tree/*bow and arrow*
bird hunting 1: *blind/bow and arrow*
bird hunting 2: *platform/bow and arrow*
boar trapping 1: fence/*spiked trap*
boar trapping 2: *pitfall/bow and arrow*
boar trapping 3: *spring-pole snare/bow and arrow*
rat trapping: *baited blind/spring-pole snare*
fruit-bat trapping: *banana-baited blind/spring-pole snare*

---

bird fence
snares

At the time when Pospisil (1963a) contacted the Kapauku, most large game had left the valley and wandered into the adjacent virgin forests, due to the spread of cultivated plots and the population density. For the same reason not one dog was left in the region. The only game still hunted were wild boar, several species of marsupials, reptiles, giant rats, and birds. Python snakes were felled from trees with *stones* and killed with *clubs*. *Clubs* were also used to kill wild boars captured by the hunters. When the grasslands were dry they were set on *fire*, and the escaping rats, marsupials, or birds were collected inside *net bags* by a group of hunters who followed the fire line. Sometimes the younger men walked ahead of the fire, killing the escaping prey with *bows and arrows*. The bow had a hardwood or palmwood shaft with a split-rattan bowstring, and a different arrow variety was used with each species of game hunted. The rat-hunting arrow was the most complex, with a six-pronged point and, not unreasonably, this most complex form was employed to hunt the only economically significant species. During floods, groups of men, women, and children stamped on the elevated, grassy ares that had become small *islands*, to force the exit of rodents.

The hunters hid behind *banana trees* to shoot with *bows and arrows* the bats that were attracted by the fruit. Birds, lured with berries, were shot from dome-shaped *blinds* made with branches and grass. The men also concealed themselves from their bird prey using *platforms* constructed between four trees.

Both in the forest and next to a cultivated garden, wild boar were trapped with *bamboo spikes*. An alternative method was to dig a *pitfall* on a boar's path and camouflage it with reeds and grass held in place with two logs. One of the most commonly used boar-trapping subsistants was a *spring-pole snare* set in the forest. It consisted of a V-shaped frame tied at the top and stabilized with an arched support. Within the resultant triangle, a rattan noose attached to the upper end of a bent spring pole hung vertically. The spring pole was bound by another rope to the trigger, an unstable twig placed across the bottom of the V-shaped frame. When a boar touched the trigger it slid off the frame, releasing the spring pole with the attached noose (Fig. 22).

A hunter, hiding inside a *blind* made of reeds and grass, lured rats with a sweet-potato *bait* that he placed on the ground in front of a *spring-pole snare*, identical

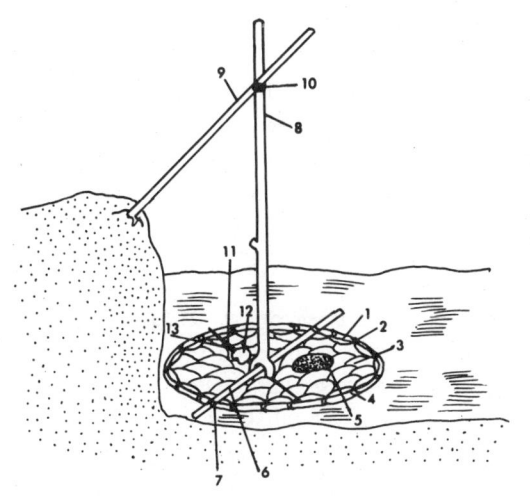

Figure 21. Kapauku Papuan baited dipnet. 1. branch frame, 2. frame grass binder, 3. inner-bark string netting, 4. netting-frame grass binder, 5. sinker, 6. wood handle, 7. frame-handle rattan binder, 8. wood forked-stick support, 9. wood anchor pole, 10. stick support-anchor-pole rattan binder, 11. bait stick, 12. sweet-potato (lizard) bait, 13. bait stick-netting grass binder. (Reprinted with permission of the Yale University Publications in Anthropology, and the author Leopold Pospisil.)

Figure 22. Kapauku Papuan boar-trapping spring-pole snare. 1. support frame, 2. support-frame rattan binder, 3. arch support, 4. arch support-frame rattan binder, 5. spring pole, 6. rattan noose, 7. spring-trigger rattan binder, 8. trigger stick. (Reprinted with permission of the Yale University Publications in Anthropology, and the author Leopold Pospisil.)

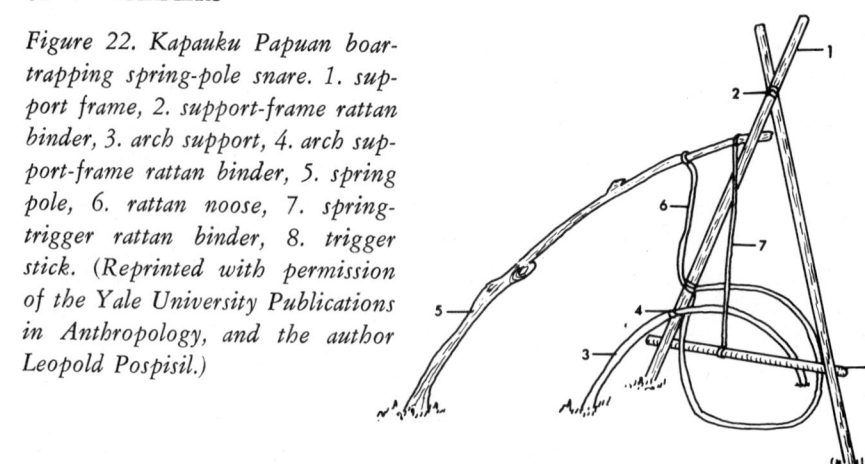

to the wild-boar facility, but smaller. Yet another *snare*, similar to the one for rats, was set to trap fruit bats lured with bananas placed inside a small *blind*. The only facilities that functioned alone were rattan snares, hung from openings on V-shaped *fences* to trap ducks or mud hens, and two *snares* placed on the circular dancing ground of courting bower birds.

Gathering

gathering frogs: three canoes/torch/*three dipnets* (hands)/three reed (bamboo) containers (bottle gourds)
gathering insects: canoe/hands/bamboo containers
gathering wasps: torch/hands

The Kapauku women collected many species of insects, amphibians, and wild plants, with aids. When the waters of a river or lake were low, three or more women went out in their *canoes* and blinded the frogs with *torches*. The frogs were then easily collected in *dipnets* or with bare *hands* and placed in *bamboo containers* or *bottle gourds* sealed with leaves. Other collective enterprises were organized by the females whenever a flood or a heavy rain inundated part of the valley. From their *canoes* they collected by *hand* the insects that floated on the grasslands and placed them in their *bamboo containers*. Gathering was also performed daily by individuals of both sexes who, on their way to their gardens, picked up bugs or caterpillars from shrubs or rotting trees. Sometimes they applied a *torch* to a wasp's nest and retrieved the roasted insects by *hand*.

Storants

According to Pospisil, the sweet potatoes could not be stored, which explains why only three storing devices were used. Water, frogs, tadpoles, larvae, and insects were kept in bottle gourds sealed with bundles of leaves. During their travels, the men stored food inside net carrying bags. The only structural storant was the feast house built by the sponsor of a pig feast.

Analysis

The total subsistant inventory of the Kapauku was numerically similar to the Ao (24) since the Kapauku possessed 22 forms. But the total number of components differed significantly, for while the Kapauku subsistants had 96 components, all Ao subsistants possessed 123 parts. Similarly to the Ao, the three Kapauku complex subsistants were used to hunt. In the sense that simple and complex subsistants were employed to take the same animal species, their hunting technology was specialized. Furthermore, the variety of hunting types was second only to that of the Point Barrow Eskimo. Ten hunting arrows were reported, three blinds, and four spring-pole snares. The technological diversity in hunting subsistants was said to be a characteristic of incipient farmers who also hunted.

Throughout the levels of economic development considered in this book, an association between hunting subsistants, complex forms, and male activities was observed. Similarly, simple, tended fishing facilities were associated with female subsistence activities. Counting the components in each Kapauku taxonomic class, the tended, simple facilities had the most components (39), of which 22 were associated with fishing, 11 with hunting, and 6 with gathering, reinforcing the correlation between simple, tended facilities and fishing. Ethnographic reports indicate that fishing was a female activity. Among the Kapauku, the fishing technology was highly developed and their most complex subsistant was a baited dipnet with 13 components, used to fish. Since the structural complexity of the Kapauku subsistants, measured by the component total (96), was lower than that of the Ao (123), perhaps the difference in complexity was due to the development of fishing forms among the Kapauku and the corresponding hunting emphasis of the Ao.

The storing technology of the Kapauku was remarkably poor, reflecting environmental obstacles to storage such as the nature of the crops, which were, reportedly, not storable. The only specialized and long-term storant was a storehouse to keep meat, and all varieties of food were kept inside the gourd and net-bag containers.

The resource variability and the continuously harvestable cultivated plants relieved the Kapauku from subsistence anxieties. If it is true that resource uncertainties may be measured with material possessions, then we would expect the ceremonial paraphernalia of the Kapauku to be insignificant. Counting together the subsistants and nonsubsistants, the Kapauku total material inventory consisted of 82 forms. The subsistants represented the largest class, with 26 percent of the total and the ceremonial objects represented the smallest class, with 15 percent of the total. These results were validated by the ethnographic reports, which stressed the extremely secular orientation of the culture.

Of the 27 technoeconomic associations, 44 percent involved hunting, 37 percent fishing, 14 percent farming, and the rest gathering and animal domestication. In Murdock (1967) the Kapauku were presumed to obtain close to 60 percent of their food from agriculture, 20 percent from animal husbandry activities, and 10 percent from hunting and fishing. Murdock's percentages do not correspond to the strategic variability observed in this study. The Kapauku had more different ways to hunt than to do anything else, but in terms of subsistants and aids, the most complex technotask was extensive-shifting cultivation, in which 17 forms were employed. Thus, the greatest technological involvement occurred in the central survival activity and was correlated with the staple, but the variability of techniques was not.

The relative percentages of subsistants and aids in association were calculated, as was done for the Ao, with the following results:

	Subsistants (in percentages)	Aids (in percentages)
farming	24	76
hunting	70	30
fishing	46	53

In both tribes, the highest percentage of aids was employed to farm and the highest percentage of subsistants to hunt. There was an inverse correlation in both activities with respect to subsistants and aids: the highest percentage of one class corresponded to the lowest of the other. Thus, the aids were more significant in the farming activities of any group, whereas the subsistants were more characteristic of hunting activities. One possible reason for this dichotomous emphasis was mentioned earlier in the section on the Ao Naga. The Kapauku data agrees remarkably with the Ao results. Thus, the suggestion that these percentages reflect different relationships between man and environment during the performance of alternative subsistence activities is restated. Aids play a more significant role when the food resources are under greater human control, whereas subsistants are the primary manufactures in uncontrolled food-procuring situations, such as wild-game hunting.

TABLE 8. AO NAGA AND KAPAUKU PAPUAN STORANTS

	Ao Naga	Kapauku Papuan
Naturefact		
receptacle		
short-term		gourd(2)
Artifact		
receptacle		
short-term	water container(1) bottle gourd(1) basket(4)	net bag(4)
long-term	bamboo tray(4)	
structure		
short-term	rice shed(2)	
long-term	water well(6) granary(7) house(25) (outer room of house) (corner main room)	storehouse(4)

TABLE 9. AO NAGA AND KAPAUKU PAPUAN SUBSISTANTS

	Ao Naga	*Kapauku Papuan*
Naturefact		
implement		
weapon		
simple		stone(1)
		club(1)
Artifact		
implement		
instrument		
simple	sickle(3)	harvesting stick(1)
	reaping basket(4)	harvesting stone knife(1)
		earth knife(1)
		reaping bag(5)
weapon		
simple	dao(3)	bamboo knife(1)
	spear(5)(1 var.)	leister(9)
complex	blowgun(4)	bow and arrow(11)(9 var.)
	bow and arrow(5)	
	crossbow(14)	
facility		
tended		
simple	halter(1)	dam(1)
	fish poison(1)(2 var.)	forked stick(1)
	boar corral(2)	baited stick(3)
	cattle compound(2)	scoop(4)
	fish dam and platform(3)	bird blind(4)(2 var.)
	fish weir(3)	dipnet(6)(4 var.)
	monkey tunnel trap(3)	bird-hunting platform(7)
	nesting basket(4)	baited dipnet(13)
	fishhook(4)	
	dipnet(5)	
untended		
simple	deer pitfall(4)	bird fence(4)(1 var.)
	elephant pitfall(4)	spiked trap(4)
	bird lime stick(4)(1 var.)	pigsty(6)
	pigsty(9)	
complex	bird fence(8)(1 var.)	boar pitfall(4)
	elephant trap(9)	boar spring-pole snare(8)(3 var.)
	monkey fall trap(9)	
	deer snare(10)(1 var.)	

CASE STUDY INTERACTIONS

1. Devise an approach that integrates social variables with the technoeconomic analysis. Suggested Case Studies to consult include: *The Two Worlds of the Washo* (Downs 1966), *Being a Palauan* (Barnett 1960), and *The Huron: Farmers of the North* (Trigger 1969). You may wish to consider the division of labor and whether the activities are individual or collective, coordinated or uncoordinated, localized or dispersed. Test the applicability of the following example or suggest a different approach.

EXAMPLE:

	Cultivation (activity)	Subsistant and Aid	Component		No. of People		Labor Unit
t	cutting down jungle	machete	3	×	10	=	30
a	turning the soil	hoe	3	×	5	=	15
s	planting	stick	1	×	6	=	6
k	harvesting	stick	1	×	2	=	2
							53

A *labor unit* results from multiplying the maximum number of people and the components of the subsistants or aids employed in each task. Adding all the labor units in an activity gives a measure of sociotechnoeconomic complexity, which may be compared with other activities performed in the same society or with those recorded for other cultures.

2. Can you think of a different manner to measure technotasks than the one used in this book? One alternative is to depart from the basic assumption that the most significant subsistants or aids were the ones most often used in any activity. For example, the spear was the main Ao Naga hunting weapon, appearing in the hunting associations more often than any other material form.

EXAMPLE:
Assume that in a given hypothetical activity, four associations were recorded having the following frequency of individual subsistants and aids:

1. $\underline{A}/\underline{F}/G$ WHERE: A = 3
2. $\underline{A}/\underline{B}/Z$ F = 2
3. $\underline{A}/\underline{F}$ G,B,Z,D,E,M = 1
4. $\underline{D}/\underline{E}/M$ AND: the subsistants are underlined

How could you use the above information to compare the same activity among several societies? What could you deduce on the basis of your results?

5
Foragers, Pastoralists, and Farmers Compared

Excellent books and detailed articles have been written on the material culture of aboriginal societies. Usual topics include the variability of manufactures found throughout the world, the differences in the raw materials used, and the processing techniques. No attempt has been made in this study to review these well-recorded aspects of technology. Instead, the main thrust has been to identify and compare the survival materials and activities of six preliterate societies. Because the sample was small, any generalizations are highly tentative, but a few are offered in the hope that they will stimulate further investigations on the material aspect of culture.

All the classes of the subsistant taxonomy, except for complex instruments and most naturefact categories, were represented (Table 1). In the introduction I mentioned that the use of naturefacts preceded the manufacture of artifacts. At the dawn of man's technological history he presumably relied largely on unmodified sticks and stones to survive. Thus, it is more remarkable that *any* naturefacts should still be used by contemporary cultures than that most naturefacts have been lost.

TABLE 10. NUMERICAL COMPARISON OF SUBSISTANT CLASSES

Subsistant Classes	Foragers	Pastoralists	Farmers	Total
simple instruments	6	4	6	16
simple weapons	8	6	6	20
complex weapons	5	4	4	13
simple tended sets	7	8	18	33
complex tended sets	2	4	0	6
simple untended sets	3	11	7	21
complex untended sets	1	3	6	10
Total	32	40	47	

The subsistant classes represented different functional possibilities, and to determine the relative employment of each class among the societies of the sample, the individual subsistants were counted. Table 10 shows that the two foraging societies, the Tiwi and Point Barrow Eskimo, used more simple weapons than any of the other people; the Tibetan and Reindeer Chukchi pastoralists used simple, untended facilities predominantly, and the Ao Naga and Kapauku farmers possessed a majority of simple, tended forms. It is reasonable that foragers should have more weapons, for killing devices are characteristic equipment of people primarily dependent on wild species. Nomads, on the other hand, did not possess an extensive killing technology, but required subsistants to keep the herds alive. Ways to hold the animals were of foremost significance and the simple, untended sets fulfilled these requirements, by definition. The prevalence of simple, tended facilities among the farmers is less easily explained, since one would expect instruments to predominate. But their simple, tended sets were far more numerous than any other class, and 10 of the 18 tended sets were used to fish. Thus, a greater portion of the horticulturalists' subsistants were employed in occupations other than farming.

The domestication of animals and plants represents one of the major achievements in man's cultural development. A proliferation of material forms is commonly believed to have followed each major economic advance and yet few, if any, anthropological studies have been directly addressed to this question. The association between the material productions of cultures and their economic level may be easily tested with the subsistant and storant taxonomies. Because of time and space limitations, only two societies were included in this study to represent each major developmental stage, but larger tests should be conducted. Counting all the subsistants of the paired societies, fewer forms were found among foragers than the other groups; the herders possessed slightly more, and the greatest number was present among the farmers. The technological complexity of the subsistants, measured by their component numbers, agreed with these results. The foragers had a total of 148 components, the herders 216, and the farmers 219 (Fig. 23). Perhaps if a larger sample were to be compared, the differences would be more significant. In the meantime, the quantity and complexity of the diverse exploitative technologies and the main subsistence activity practiced appear to be correlated. However, the numerical increase was not directly related to the focal economy of a culture, as attested by the proliferation of fishing facilities among the farmers.

The division of subsistants into implements and facilities was presumed to be highly significant in technological and cultural terms. If the dichotomy is valid, then we would expect peoples whose subsistence base differed to employ these survival productions differently. Components were presumed to be more accurate indexes of complexity than the subsistant types; therefore, rather than the types, the relative component numbers of implements and facilities were counted (Fig. 23). The foragers had more components among the implements than among the facilities. The herders and farmers, on the other hand, had more facility components, except for Tibet, where the totals for both classes were almost identical. The Point Barrow Eskimo hunters had the greatest number of implement components, and the Chukchi herders possessed more facility components than any other

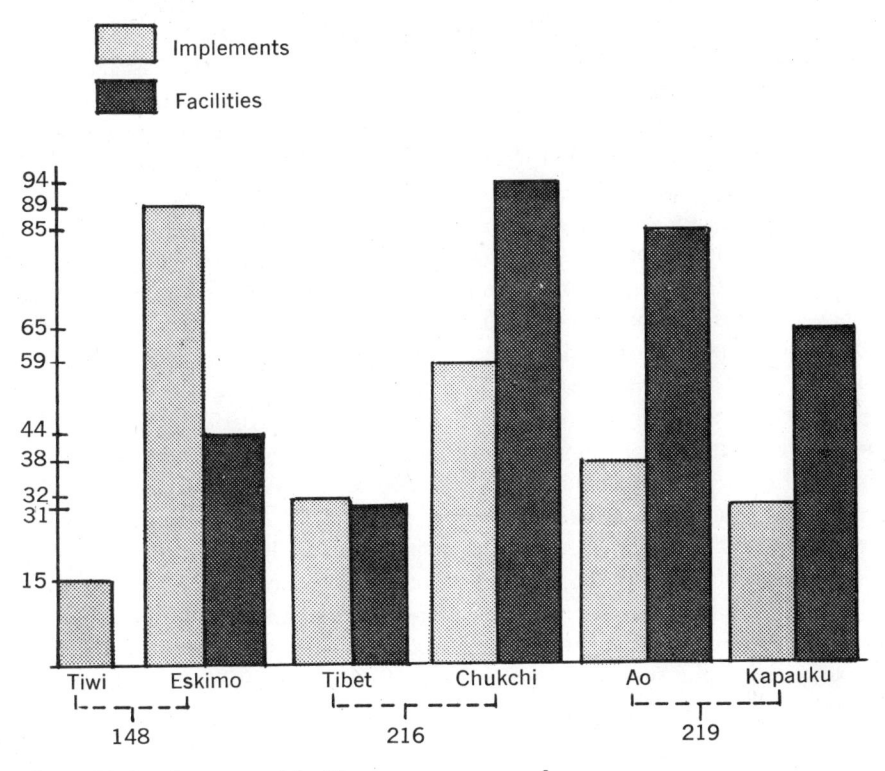

Figure 23. Implement and facility component numbers.

group. These two peoples shared more environmental similarities than the other societies treated in this book; both lived in the arctic—one in Alaska, and the other in Siberia. The Eskimo component total reflected their adaptation to a foraging way of life in an arctic setting, whereas the Chukchi total showed that the dependence on domesticated herds in the same environment resulted in a subsistant assemblage with more complex facilities than implements.

While the subsistants represented the material inventory for survival, the technotasks referred to the actual strategies. *Each tribe had an almost identical number of subsistants and technotasks.* Thus, by knowing the total number of subsistants of a society, we may be able to assess its economic diversification, whereas if we know the total number of associations, we may be able to predict the number of subsistants possessed.

All the sampled cultures, except the Tibetan, had a greater percentage of hunting technotasks than any other activity. The Tibetans had more animal husbandry associations, but it must be remembered that the foraging information for these people was considered inadequate. Thus, in the sample, *regardless of the dominant subsistence activity of a culture, more strategies were employed to hunt than to do anything else.* Two possible reasons may have been the greater habitat variability associated with wild game, and the sedentariness required with domestication. The most complex subsistants found among each tribe were employed to forage for food. The Eskimo used the toggle-headed harpoon to hunt seals and the Tiwi used the ax to gather wild foods. Similarly, the most complex subsistant found among herders and farmers was not used to herd or farm, but to hunt or fish. Apparently, aboriginal societies expended the greatest effort in hunting, both in terms of strategic variability and technological complexity.

The subsistence activities may be compared cross culturally by counting the total number of subsistants and aids used in each association. The greater the total number, the more complex the activity is presumed to be. Among all the peoples studied, except the Tiwi, the most complex activity was related to their main food source. This was evidenced by seal hunting among the Point Barrow Eskimo; the movement of the Tibetan and Chukchi herds; the cultivation of rice among the Ao; and the Kapauku extensive-shifting cultivation of sweet potatoes.

Because of the length of this study, not all the concepts considered were refined to the fullest extent. The following are suggestions on how the approach may be broadened to integrate technology with other sociocultural aspects. Figure 1 (p. 3) illustrates the units of analysis and their relationships. The tasks and the material forms used in the associations are at the same conceptual level, but the tasks were not divided comparably to the subsistants, into components, primarily because the emphasis of the book was the material culture. Yet, a task such as caribou hunting may be identified by several social components. Among these are the number of people required, the chracteristics of the task force (whether it is young or old, male or female), and the organizational features, such as individual versus collective, or coordinated versus uncoordinated. Either one of these variables may be selected to assess the complexity of tasks, or a composite index may be devised based on two or more social measures. To illustrate how the social variables may be integrated with the technology, I have provided an example (p. 66) for the Case Study Interaction 1, Chapter 4, in which the task is measured by the number of people involved, and the interrelationship between tasks and artifacts is represented by a *labor unit*.

Throughout the book, where appropriate, I have pointed out the sociocultural implications of the technoeconomic patterns. Future research may be based on the factors that seem to covary most directly with the subsistants and the technotasks. A strong relationship was apparent between the sex of the most productive unit of a society and the general characteristics of the technology. In the chapter on foragers the most evident relationships were found between simple subsistants and a predominantly female productive core, and complex subsistants and a male-centered economic organization. Additional factors were presumed to link certain behavioral patterns with technology. Cooking, which is an almost exclusively female activity, appeared to explain the greater knowledge of containers possessed by the women and their prevalent use of facilities.

The relatively new field of ethnoscience, that attempts to understand cultures from the point of view of the natives, provides a perspective that should prove valuable when studying manufactures. Although only briefly considered, it was possible in this study to assign different conceptions of time to the early inventors of storage containers and subsistants. The search for the relationships between the native classifications of subsistence foods and the subsistant classes employed to obtain them should enrich this particular approach to culture.

In the text I referred to the relationhip between the material culture and ceremonialism. Apparently, the emphasis on ritual and the complexity of the ceremonial equipment are directly correlated and both seem to be related to food-quest uncertainties. It is quite likely that the ceremonial paraphernalia of a sample of societies, their ceremonial elaborations, and the predictability of their main resources are highly correlated.

The technotasks or survival strategies of six preliterate people, rather than their subsistants, were the main subjects of this book because the technotasks are a better index of the economic focus of a culture. Our understanding of the material aspect of man's adaptation to his physical environment may be extended through the technotask approach. Suggestively, similar technological associations would be expected in similar environments. This and other proposals of an ecological nature may be easily analyzed with the approach presented in this book. By looking at the subsistants through their economic functions, a more dynamic aspect of the technology was disclosed than is usual with traditional treatments. However, this type of study has a long road to travel, and that road is as long as man's dependence on the materials he fashions.

Glossary

Activity: The broadest unit considered in this book. It refers to the functional context of the subsistence pursuits. Operationally, an activity includes the technotasks within one main economic division. For example, all technotasks that procure wild game belong to the hunting activity. *See also* technotask.
Aid: Any natural or artificial form employed in association with a subsistant in order to harvest wild or domestic foods. Some natural aids, for example hands, function like subsistants, but they are classed as aids because they are not material but anatomical forms. Transportation devices are commonly occurring aids.
Artifact: Any manufactured object which requires processing skills and becomes a possession of its maker.
Association: The simultaneous or serial employment of two or more forms, either subsistants or a combination of subsistants and aids, to fulfill one subsistence task. An example is a fishing net set in a dammed river.
Complex Form: A subsistant, such as the bow and arrow, with component parts that move during its employment and that functions through the application of a mechanical principle.
Component: A discrete, functional element of a material form. By definition decorative elements are excluded, except when they are also functionally essential. For example, a knife may have three components: a stone blade, a wooden shaft, and the fiber binding the blade to the shaft. When the components of a subsistant are functionally equivalent, they are considered as one, as in the case of a dam built by piling many rocks across a river. However, a corral made up of multiple stakes and bushes has a component complexity of two. Each material is considered to be functionally distinct.
Facility: A predominantly stationary subsistant that passively awaits the prey and does not require muscular energy to function. A facility attracts, contains, holds, or restrains the animal prey. No facility is used to harvest plant products. A classical example is a pitfall.
Implement: A subsistant requiring the direct exertion of human energy to obtain plant or animal foods such as a sickle, and a bow and arrow.
Instrument: One subdivision of the implement category including subsistants only used to collect species incapable of motion, such as plants. A digging stick is the prime example.
Long-Term Storant: A storing device that keeps food for long periods of time, exemplified by rice granaries.
Naturefact: A natural object extracted from its environmental context and used without prior modification to obtain food, such as a stone thrown at a bird.
Preartifact: A distinction mainly offered to stress an evolutionary point. A preartifact represents an intermediate stage in the development of technology, lying somewhere between the use of unmodified naturefacts and the manufac-

ture of patterned artifacts. Tentatively, this stage may be considered to have been reached when the first processing techniques began to be applied to the natural forms, and the resultant manufactures were discarded after one or two usages. Suggestively, this stage serves to separate the technological achievements of animals from those of men. In his evolutionary history, *Homo sapiens* must have passed through a preartifactual stage before entering the technological age, attained when true artifacts began to be made.

Receptacle: One of the two divisions of the storant category, referring to devices that confine food products closely, such as pottery vessels or a pit dug in the snow.

Short-Term Storant: A storing device to keep food temporarily, such as the branches of a tree on which meat is hung.

Simple Form: Any subsistant whose component parts do not move while being employed and which may consist of only one component, like a club.

Storant: A natural or material form used to store food, be it temporarily or for long periods of time.

Structure: One of the two divisions of the storant category, which includes forms that contain food loosely and may serve other purposes besides food storage, such as a tent.

Subsistant: The naturefacts and artifacts used by preliterate men to procure food directly. Only those forms which serve to satisfy human caloric requirements are included. A harpoon and a fishhook are examples.

Task: A component of an activity, representing the functional context of an association. For example, caribou hunting is a task within the more general activity "to hunt."

Technotask: A concept integrating the subsistence materials with the tasks. Thus, the ax used by a woman to cut down a honey nest, the brush employed to extricate the food, and the actual operations performed by the woman in using these objects, represent the honey gathering technotask.

Tended Set: A subsistant facility that requires a human presence to function. An example is a dipnet held by a fisherwoman standing on a river bank.

Untended Set: A facility that works in the absence of men, such as a trap set in a forest.

Weapon: An implement which injures or kills the mobile prey, such as a spear, a knife, a boomerang.

References

Antropova, V. V., and V.G. Kuznetsova, 1964, "The Chukchi," in *The Peoples of Siberia*, M. G. Levin, and L. P. Potapov, eds., pp. 799–835. Chicago: University of Chicago Press. (Orig., 1956).

Balfour, H., 1917, "Some Types of Native Hoes, Naga Hills," *Man*, 74:105–108.

Basedow, Herbert, 1913, "Notes on the Natives of Bathurst Island, North Australia," *Journal of the Royal Anthropological Institute*, Vol. 43.

———, 1925, *The Australian Aboriginal*. Adelaide: F. W. Preece and Sons.

Berndt, Ronald M., and Catherine H. Berndt, 1964, *The World of the First Australians: An Introduction to the Traditional Life of the Australian Aborigines*. Sydney: Ure Smith.

Bogoras, Waldemar, 1904–1909, "The Chukchee," *Jesup North Pacific Expedition*, Vol. 7 (3 parts). American Museum of Natural History, Memoirs, No. 11, Pt. 1. Leiden, Netherlands.

Brues, Alice, 1959, "The Spearman and the Archer: An Essay on Selection in Body Build," *American Anthropologist*, 61:457–469.

Chance, Norman, 1966, *The Eskimo of North Alaska*. Case Studies in Cultural Anthropology. George and Louise Spindler, eds. New York: Holt, Rinehart and Winston, Inc.

Downs, James F., and Robert B. Ekvall, 1965, "Animals and Social Types in the Exploitation of the Tibetan Plateau," in *Man, Culture and Animals: The Role of Animals in Human Ecological Adjustments*, Anthony Leeds and Andrew P. Vayda, eds., pp. 169–184. American Association for the Advancement of Science. Publication No. 78. Washington, D.C.

Ekvall, Robert B., 1968, *Fields on the Hoof: Nexus of Tibetan Nomadic Pastoralism*. Case Studies in Cultural Anthropology. George and Louise Spindler, eds. New York: Holt, Rinehart and Winston, Inc.

Fraser, Sir James, 1922, "The Use of the Bow among the Naga Tribes of Assam," *Folklore*, 33:305–306.

Fürer-Haimendorf, Christoph von, 1969, *The Konyak Nagas: An Indian Frontier Tribe*. Case Studies in Cultural Anthropology. George and Louise Spindler, eds. New York: Holt, Rinehart and Winston, Inc.

Godden, Gertrud M., 1898, "Naga and other Frontier Tribes of Northeast India," *Journal of the Royal Anthropological Institute*, 27:2–52.

Goodale, Jane, 1957, "Alonga Bush: A Tiwi Hunt," *University Museum Bulletin*, Vol. 21, No. 3. Pennsylvania University.

———, 1971, "Tiwi Wives: A Study of the Women of Melville Island, North Australia," *American Ethnological Society*, Monograph No. 51.

Harney, W. E., and A. P. Elkin, 1943, "Melville and Bathurst Islanders: A Short Description," *Oceania*, 13:228–234.

Hart, C. W. M., and Arnold R. Pilling, 1960, *The Tiwi of North Australia*. Case Studies in Cultural Anthropology. George and Louise Spindler, eds. New York: Holt, Rinehart and Winston, Inc.

Hermanns, Matthias, 1949, *Die Nomaden von Tibet: die Sozial-Wirtschaftlichen*

REFERENCES

Grundlagen der Hirtenkulturen in Amdo und von Inner-Asien. Ursprung und Entwicklung der Viehzucht. Wien: Verlag Herold.
Hockett, Charles, 1960, "The Origin of Speech," *Scientific American*, 203:88–96.
Hutton, J. H., 1921, *The Sema Nagas.* New York: Macmillan.
Lantis, Margaret, 1947, "Alaskan Eskimo Ceremonialism," *American Ethnological Society*, Monograph No. 11. New York: Augustin.
Leeds, Anthony, 1965, "Reindeer Herding and Chukchi Social Institutions," in *Man, Culture and Animals: The Role of Animals in Human Ecological Adjustments.* Anthony Leeds and Andrew P. Vayda, eds., pp. 87–128. American Association for the Advancement of Science. Publication No. 78. Washington, D.C.
Mills, J. P., 1926, *The Ao Nagas.* New York: Macmillan.
Mullan, C. S., 1932, "Report on Assam," *Census of India*, Vol. III, Pt. 1.
Murdoch, John, 1892, "Ethnological Results of the Point Barrow Expedition," *Bureau of Ethnology, Ninth Annual Report*, pp. 3–441. Washington, D.C.: U.S. Government Printing Office.
Murdock, George Peter, 1967, *Ethnographic Atlas.* Pittsburgh: University of Pittsburgh Press.
Nath Majumdar, Surendra, 1924, "The Ao Nagas," *Man in India*, 4:28.
Nelson, Richard, 1969, *Hunters of the Northern Ice.* Chicago: University of Chicago Press.
Oswalt, Wendell H., 1967, *Alaskan Eskimos.* San Francisco: Chandler Publishing Co.
———, 1973, *Habitat and Technology: The Evolution of Hunting.* New York: Holt, Rinehart, and Winston, Inc.
Peale, S. E., 1874, "The Nagas and Neighboring Tribes," *Journal of the Royal Anthropological Institute*, 3:476–481.
Pospisil, Leopold, 1963a, "Kapauku Papuan Economy," *Yale University Publications in Anthropology*, No. 67. New Haven.
———, 1963b, *The Kapauku Papuans of West New Guinea.* Case Studies in Cultural Anthropology. George and Louise Spindler, eds. New York: Holt, Rinehart and Winston, Inc.
Ray, P. H., 1885, "Ethnographic Sketch of the Natives of Point Barrow," *Report of the International Polar Expedition to Point Barrow, Alaska*, pp. 35–87. Washington, D.C.: U.S. Government Printing Office.
Rockhill, William Woodville, 1894, *Diary of a Journey through Mongolia and Tibet in 1891 and 1892.* Smithsonian Institution, Washington, D.C.
———, 1895, "Notes on the Ethnology of Tibet Based on the Collections in the United States National Museum. *U.S. National Museum Report for the Year Ending June 30, 1893*, pp. 665–749. Washington, D.C.: U.S. Government Printing Office.
Simpson, John, 1875, "Observations on the Western Eskimo and the Country They Inhabit," *A Selection of Papers on Arctic Geography and Ethnology*, pp. 233–275. London: J. Murray.
Smith, William Carlson, 1925, *The Ao Naga Tribe of Assam: A Study in Ethnology and Sociology.* New York: Macmillan.
Spencer, Baldwin, 1914, *Native Tribes of the Northern Territory of Australia.* New York: Macmillan.
Spencer, Robert F., 1959, "The North Alaskan Eskimo: A Study in Ecology and Society," *Bureau of American Ethnology, Bulletin 171.* Washington, D.C.: U.S. Government Printing Office.
Stubel, Hans, 1958, "The Mewu Fantzu: A Tibetan Tribe of Kansu," *Behavior Science Translations.* New Haven: Human Relations Area Files Press.
Trotter, H., 1887, "Account of the Pundit's Journey in Great Tibet from Leh in Ladákh to Llása and of his Return to India via Assam," *Journey of the Royal Geographical Society*, 47:86–136.

Relevant Case Studies[*]

(All studies listed below are from the Case Studies in Cultural Anthropology, except Wolcott's, which is from the series Case Studies in Education and Culture.)

Barnett, H. G., 1960, *Being a Palauan*. The fishing and farming activities of these Micronesian people are described, with detailed information on the sexual division of labor providing some of the facts needed to attempt Case Study Interaction 1, Chapter 4.

Beals, Alan R., 1962, *Gopalpur: A South Indian Village*. The plow agriculture practiced by the sedentary south Indian farmers of Gopalpur may be compared with the plow agriculture practiced in the Mexican village of Tepoztlán using the concepts in this unit.

Dentan, Robert Knox, 1968, *The Semai: A Nonviolent People of Malaya*. Case Study Interaction 3, Chapter 2 may be attempted with the data on the hunting and fishing activities of the Semai. The excellent discussion on the native classification of the biological world allows the test of a possible relationship between the material culture, as defined in this book, and the Semai taxonomy on the species procured.

Diamond, Norma, 1969, *Kun Shen: A Taiwan Village*. This Case Study provides detailed information on the technology, working force, and seasonality in a contemporary village and may be used to expand some of the concepts presented in this unit.

Downs, James, 1966, *The Two Worlds of the Washo*. This Case Study has more technoeconomic details than most books in the series and it is very useful in several contexts: (a) to attempt the Case Study Interaction 1, Chapter 2, using the material culture information; (b) to solve Case Study Interaction 2, Chapter 2, with the excellent account on acculturation; and (c) to devise the model suggested in Case Study Interaction 1, Chapter 4 with the data on the social aspects of subsistence.

———, 1972, *The Navajo*. Downs makes detailed observations on multiple aspects of pastoralism, such as the methods of teaching herding to children, the operations performed on each species tended, the care of the animals, the relationship between a family and its herd, and even the attitude towards falling off a horse. This is a useful source to solve Case Study Interactions 1 and 2, Chapter 3.

Ekvall, Robert B., 1968, *Fields on the Hoof: Nexus of Tibetan Nomadic Pastoralism*. This Case Study is more explicitly concerned with ecological adaptations than most. The descriptions of the influence of the high-altitude envi-

---

[*] These are edited by George and Louise Spindler, and published by Holt, Rinehart and Winston, Inc.

ronment on the material culture of the aBrog pastoralists make this an excellent reference for Case Study Interaction 2, Chapter 3.

Fürer-Haimendorf, Christoph von, 1969, *The Konyak Nagas: An Indian Frontier Tribe*. The Konyak Nagas are closely related to the Ao Naga tribe described in this Unit. From the sections on the material culture and the ecological relationships and social consequences of slash-and-burn cultivation, it is possible to obtain the information necessary to attempt the Case Study Interaction 2, Chapter IV.

Hoebel, Adamson E., 1960, *The Cheyennes: Indians of the Great Plains*. Bison hunting was the main subsistence activity of this recently nomadic Great Plains group. The material culture information allows a test to be made of the hypothesis in Case Study Interaction 3, Chapter 2.

Klima, George J., 1970, *The Barabaig: East African Cattle-Herders*. Essentially, *Technology: Strategies for Survival* focuses on the main problem-solving activities of preliterate groups. Klima's approach to the cattle-herding economy of the Barabaig is similarly based on the concept that behavior patterns develop in order to solve certain problems. The sections entitled "The Problem of Land," "The Problem of Water," and "The Problem of Grazing," refer to adaptive strategies and may be used to devise a new classification of herders' activities, based on ecological criteria (Case Study Interaction 2, Chapter 3).

Lewis, Oscar, 1960, *Tepoztlán: Village in Mexico*. The excellent discussion on the practice of hoe and plow agriculture in Tepoztlán, and of the various correlates, such as amount and time of work required, productivity and population numbers, make this an ideal reference for the study of one particular aspect of subsistence: agriculture in this case. Few Case Studies illustrate as convincingly that differences in productivity, labor, and activities have a technological base.

Trigger, Bruce G., 1969, *The Huron: Farmers of the North*. The sexual division of labor is emphasized and the elaborate treatment of the subsistence activities of these northern farmers provides the raw data needed to study the relationship between the material culture and the social structure as suggested in Case Study Interaction 1, Chapter 4.

Williams, Thomas Rhys, 1965, *The Dusun: A North Borneo Society*. The association of ceremonialism with farming activities may be demonstrated using this Case Study, in which the agricultural cycle is described in conjunction with the pertinent rituals.

Wolcott, Harry F., 1967, *A Kwakiutl Village and School*. Describes contemporary life in a Northwest Coast village subsisting on a fishing and clamming economy. Wolcott stresses the changes, caused by the cash economy and the commercial fishing, on the sexual division of labor as well as the relationship between the activities, the technology, the amounts of food tapped, and the length of time spent to procure it. This Case Study may be used together with *The Two Worlds of the Washo* (Downs 1966) to devise the model referred to in Case Study Interaction 2, Chapter 2.

DATE DUE			
MAR 16 '78			
MAR 30 '78			
APR 16 '78			
GAYLORD			PRINTED IN U S A